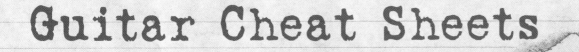

Guitar Cheat Sheets

TOP HITS

44 Mega-Hits in Musical Shorthand

ISBN 978-1-4234-9412-6

7777 W. BLUEMOUND RD. P.O. BOX 13819 MILWAUKEE, WI 53213

Visit Hal Leonard Online at
www.halleonard.com

Contents

Airplanes

Words and Music by Bobby Ray Simmons Jr., Alexander Grant, Jeremy Dussolliety, Tim Sommers and Justin Franks

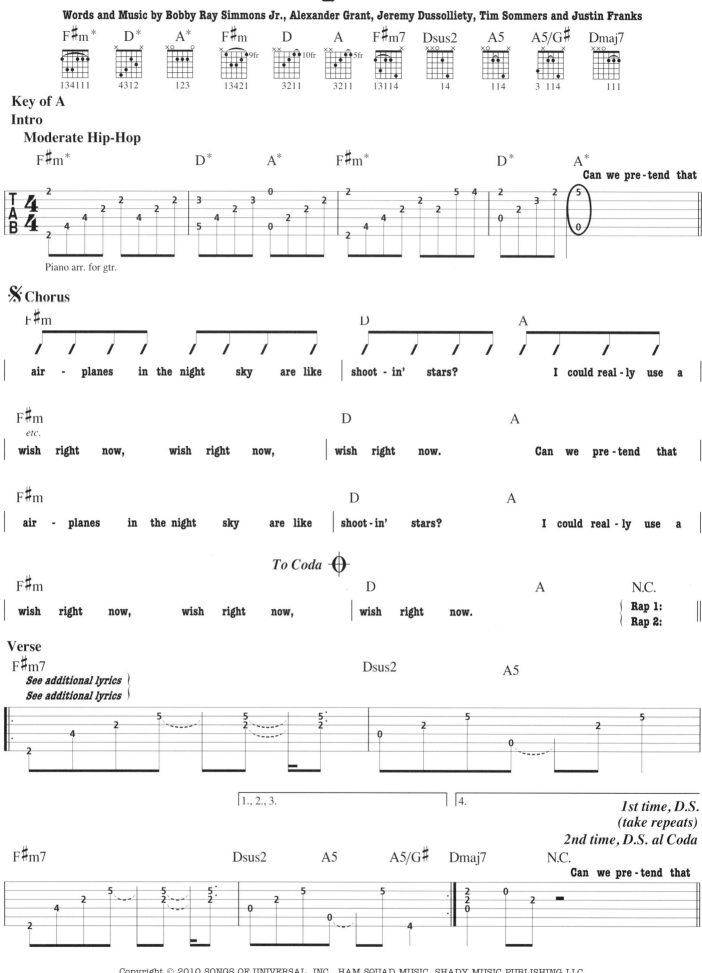

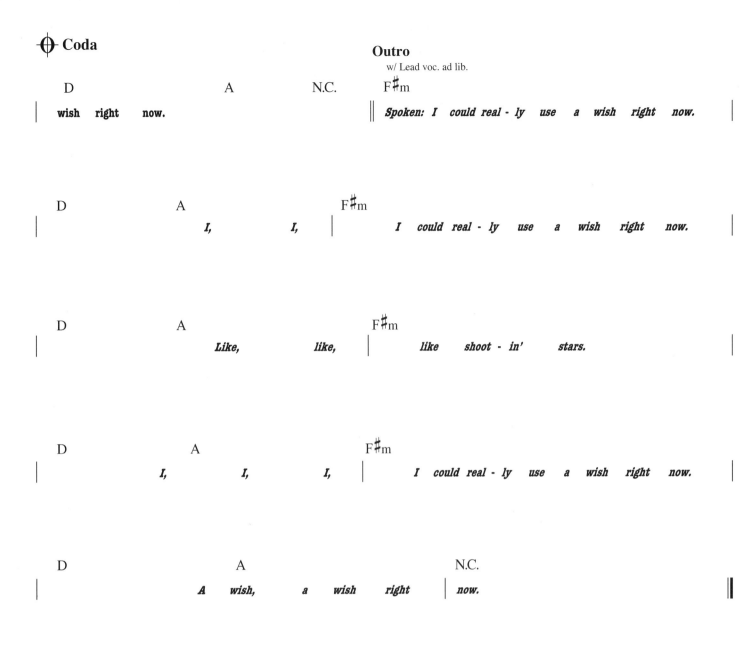

Additional Lyrics

Rap 1:

Yeah, I could use a dream or a genie or a wish to go back to a place much simpler than this.
'Cause after all the partyin' and smashin' and crashin', and all the glitz and the glam and the fashion,
And all the pandemonium and all the madness, there comes a time where you fade to the blackness.
And when you starin' at that phone in your lap, and you hopin', but them people never call you back.
But that's just how the story unfolds, you get another hand soon after you fold.
And when your plans unravel in the sand, what would you wish for if you had one chance?
So, airplane, airplane, sorry I'm late. I'm on my way, so don't close that gate.
If I don't make that then I'll switch my flight and I'll be right back at it by the end of the night.

Rap 2:

Yeah, yeah, somebody take me back to the days before this was a job, before I got paid.
Before it ever mattered what I had in my bank, yeah, back when I was tryin' to get a tip at Subway.
And back when I was rappin' for the hell of it, but now-a-days we rappin' to stay relevant.
I'm guessin' that if we can make some wishes outta airplanes, then maybe, yo, maybe I'll go back to the days
Before the politics that we call the rap game, and back when ain't nobody listen to my mix tape,
And back before I tried to cover up my slang. But this is for Decatur, what's up Bobby Ray?
So can I get a wish to end the politics and get back to the music that started this sh*t?
So here I stand, and then again I say I'm hopin' we can make some wishes outta airplanes.

All the Right Moves

Words and Music by Ryan Tedder

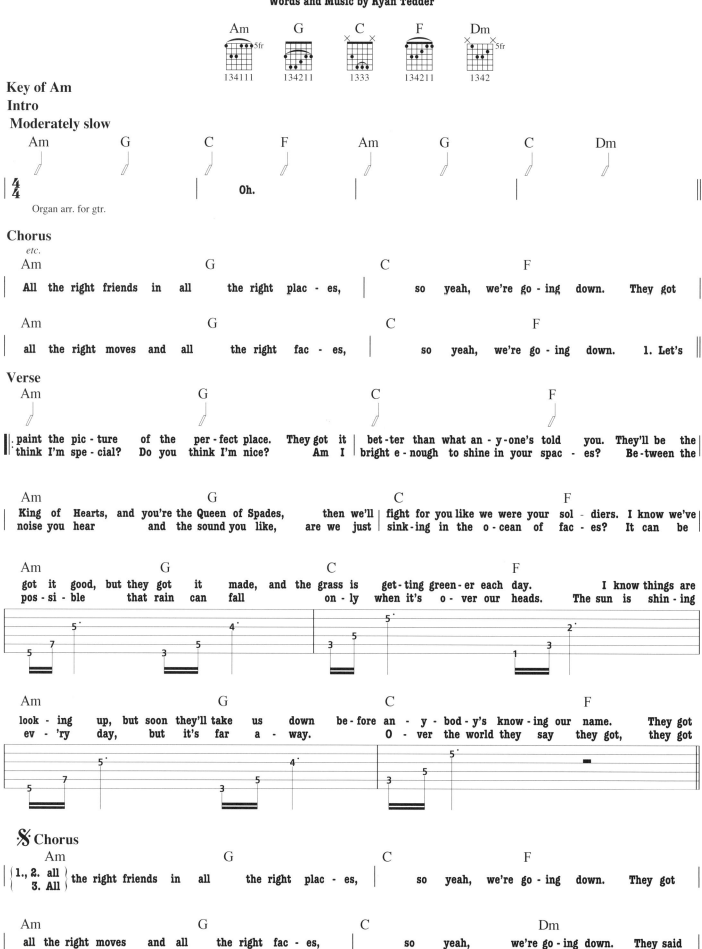

Key of Am
Intro
Moderately slow

Organ arr. for gtr.

Chorus
etc.

All the right friends in all the right plac - es, so yeah, we're go - ing down. They got all the right moves and all the right fac - es, so yeah, we're go - ing down. 1. Let's

Verse

1. paint the pic - ture of the per - fect place. They got it bet - ter than what an - y - one's told you. They'll be the
2. think I'm spe - cial? Do you think I'm nice? Am I bright e - nough to shine in your spac - es? Be - tween the

King of Hearts, and you're the Queen of Spades, then we'll fight for you like we were your sol - diers. I know we've
noise you hear and the sound you like, are we just sink - ing in the o - cean of fac - es? It can be

got it good, but they got it made, and the grass is get - ting green - er each day. I know things are
pos - si - ble that rain can fall on - ly when it's o - ver our heads. The sun is shin - ing

look - ing up, but soon they'll take us down be - fore an - y - bod - y's know - ing our name. They got
ev - 'ry day, but it's far a - way. O - ver the world they say they got, they got

𝄋 Chorus

1., 2. all } the right friends in all the right plac - es, so yeah, we're go - ing down. They got
3. All

all the right moves and all the right fac - es, so yeah, we're go - ing down. They said

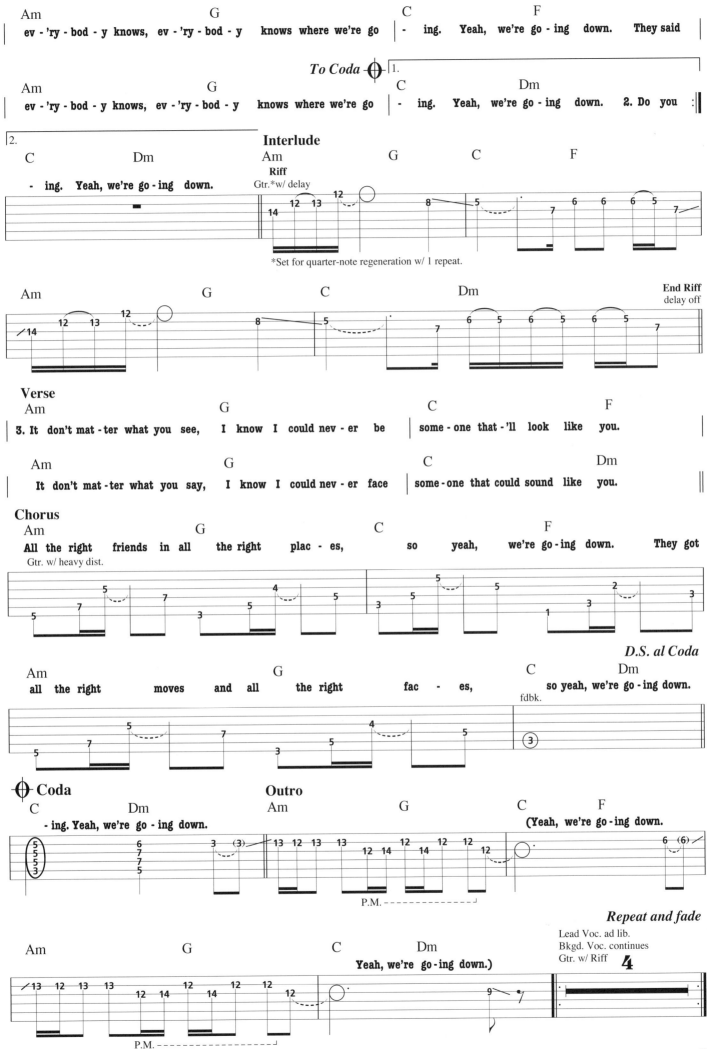

Apologize

Words and Music by Ryan Tedder

Cm   A♭maj13   E♭   Gm7/D

Key of Cm

Intro

Moderately slow, in 2

Cm   A♭maj13

Piano arr. for gtr.
w/ pick & fingers

E♭   1. Gm7/D   2. Gm7/D

(Hey,   hey,   hey.   hey,   1. I'm

Verse

Cm	A♭maj13	E♭	Gm7/D	
hold - in' on your rope, got me	ten feet off the ground.			And I'm
take an - oth - er chance, take a	fall. Take a shot for you.			I
hey.)				

Cm	A♭maj13	E♭	Gm7/D	
hear - in' what you say, but I	just can't make a sound.			You
need you like a heart needs a	beat, but it's noth - in' new,	yeah,	yeah.	I

Cm	A♭maj13	E♭	Gm7/D	
tell me that you need me,	then you go and cut me down,	but wait.		You
loved you with a fire	red, now it's turn - in'	blue, and you say		

Cm	A♭maj13	E♭	*N.C.	
tell me that you're sor - ry,	did - n't think I'd turn a - round	and say	that it's
sor - ry like an an - gel	heav - en let me think was you.	But, I'm a - fraid	it's

*2nd time, Gm7/D

Chorus

Cm	A♭maj13	E♭	Gm7/D	
too late to 'pol - o - gize.		It's too late.		I said it's

Cm   **A♭maj13**   *To Coda* ⊕   **E♭**   **Gm7/D**

| too late to 'pol - o - gize. | It's | too late.   (Hey, | hey,   hey. |

D.S. al Coda

Cm   **A♭maj13**   **E♭**   **Gm7/D**

| | | Hey, | hey,   **2.** I'd ‖

⊕ **Coda**

E♭   **Gm7/D**

| too   late, | whoa,   whoa. ‖

Interlude

Cm   **A♭maj13**   **E♭**   **Gm7/D**

| | | (Hey, | hey,   hey. |

Cm   **A♭maj13**   **E♭**   **Gm7/D**

| | | Hey, | hey,   hey.) | It's ‖

Chorus

Cm   **A♭maj13**   **E♭**   **Gm7/D**

| too late to 'pol - o - gize. | It's | too late. | I said it's |

Cm   **A♭maj13**   **E♭**   **Gm7/D**

| too late to 'pol - o - gize. | It's | too late. | I said it's |

Cm   **A♭maj13**   **E♭**   **Gm7/D**

| too late to 'pol - o - gize, | yeah. | I said it's |

Cm   **A♭maj13**   **E♭**   **Gm7/D**

| too late to 'pol - o - gize, | yeah. | I'm ‖

Outro
Freely

Cm   **A♭maj13**   **E♭**

| hold - in' on your rope, got me | ten feet off the ground. | ‖

Are You Gonna Be My Girl

Words and Music by Cameron Muncey and Nicholas Cester

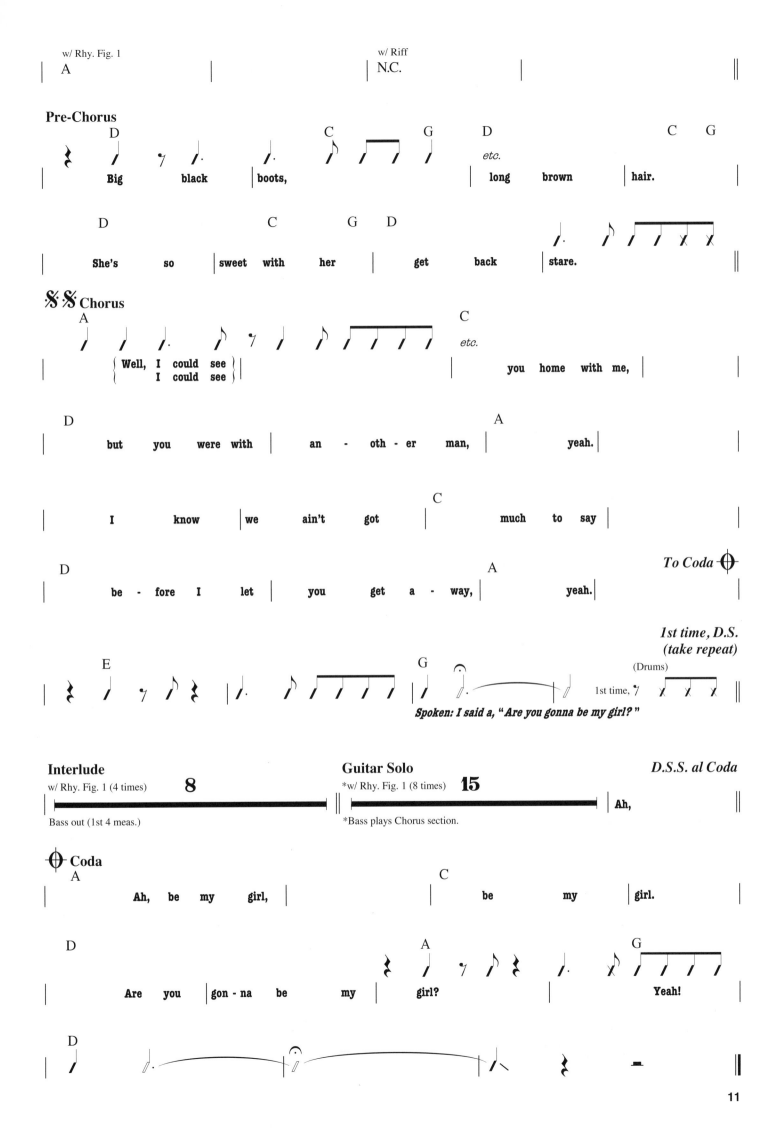

Baby

Words and Music by Justin Bieber, Christopher Stewart, Christine Flores, Christopher Bridges and Terius Nash

12

Chorus

Eb* Cm7 *etc.*

| "Ba - by, ba - by, ba | - by, oh, like | ba - by, ba - by, ba - |

Abmaj9

| - by, no, like | ba - by, ba - by, ba | - by, oh, |

Bb* Eb*

| thought you'd al - ways be mine, | mine. | Ba - by, ba - by, ba - |

Cm7

| - by, oh, like | ba - by, ba - by, ba | - by, no, like |

Abmaj9 Bb* *To Coda* ⊕

| ba - by, ba - by, ba | - by, oh, | thought you'd al - ways be mine, ‖

1.
| mine." 2. Oh, for :‖

2. *D.S. al Coda*
mine." ‖

⊕ **Coda**

Outro
w/ Intro pattern
Eb

| mine." | Yeah, yeah, yeah, | yeah, yeah, yeah. |
| (I'm gone, | | well, I'm all gone. |

Cm

| Yeah, yeah, yeah, | yeah, yeah, yeah. | Yeah, yeah, yeah, | yeah, yeah, gone, |
| Now I'm all gone, | | now I'm all gone. |

Ab

Bb Eb* Ebsus4 Eb*

| gone, gone, | gone. | |
| I'm gone.) |

Additional Lyrics

Rap 3: *When I was thirteen, I had my first love. There was nobody that compared*
To my baby, and nobody came between us or could ever come above.
She had me going crazy, oh, I was starstruck. She woke me up daily,
Don't need no Starbucks. She made my heart pound, it skip a beat when I
See her in the street and at school on the playground. But I really want to
See her on a weekend. She knows she got me dazing, 'cause she was so amazing,
And now my heart is breaking. But I just keep on saying...

Bad Day

Words and Music by Daniel Powter

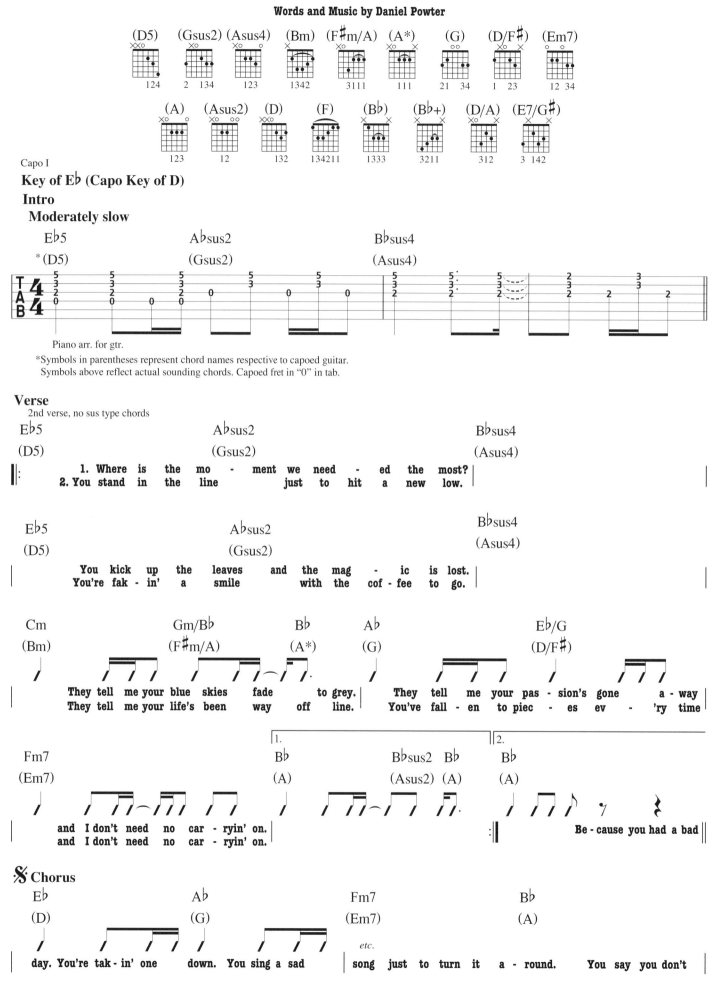

Capo I

Key of E♭ (Capo Key of D)

Intro

Moderately slow

Piano arr. for gtr.

*Symbols in parentheses represent chord names respective to capoed guitar.
Symbols above reflect actual sounding chords. Capoed fret in "0" in tab.

Verse

2nd verse, no sus type chords

E♭5	A♭sus2	B♭sus4
(D5)	(Gsus2)	(Asus4)

1. Where is the mo - ment we need - ed the most?
2. You stand in the line just to hit a new low.

E♭5	A♭sus2	B♭sus4
(D5)	(Gsus2)	(Asus4)

You kick up the leaves and the mag - ic is lost.
You're fak - in' a smile with the cof - fee to go.

Cm	Gm/B♭	B♭	A♭	E♭/G
(Bm)	(F♯m/A)	(A*)	(G)	(D/F♯)

They tell me your blue skies fade to grey. They tell me your pas - sion's gone a - way
They tell me your life's been way off line. You've fall - en to piec - es ev - 'ry time

Fm7	1. B♭	2. B♭sus2 B♭	B♭
(Em7)	(A)	(Asus2) (A)	(A)

and I don't need no car - ryin' on.
and I don't need no car - ryin' on. Be - cause you had a bad

𝄋 Chorus

E♭	A♭	Fm7	B♭
(D)	(G)	(Em7)	(A)

etc.

day. You're tak - in' one down. You sing a sad song just to turn it a - round. You say you don't

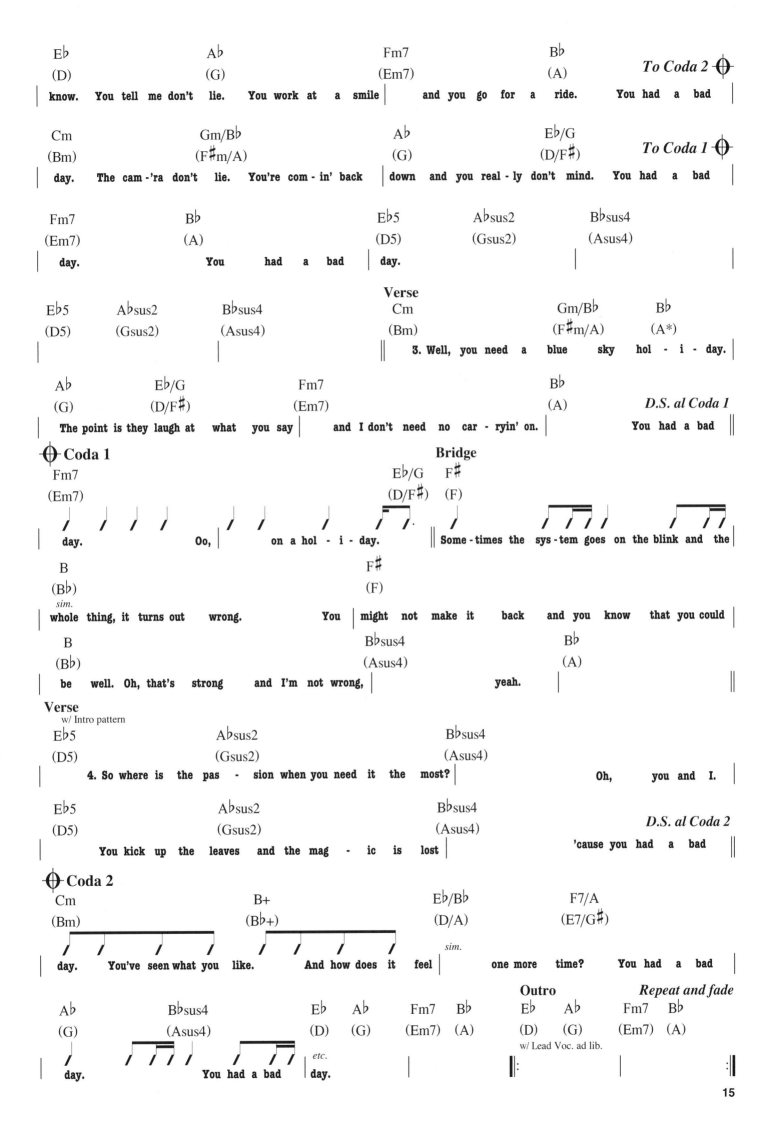

15

Bad Romance

Words and Music by Stefani Germanotta and Nadir Khayat

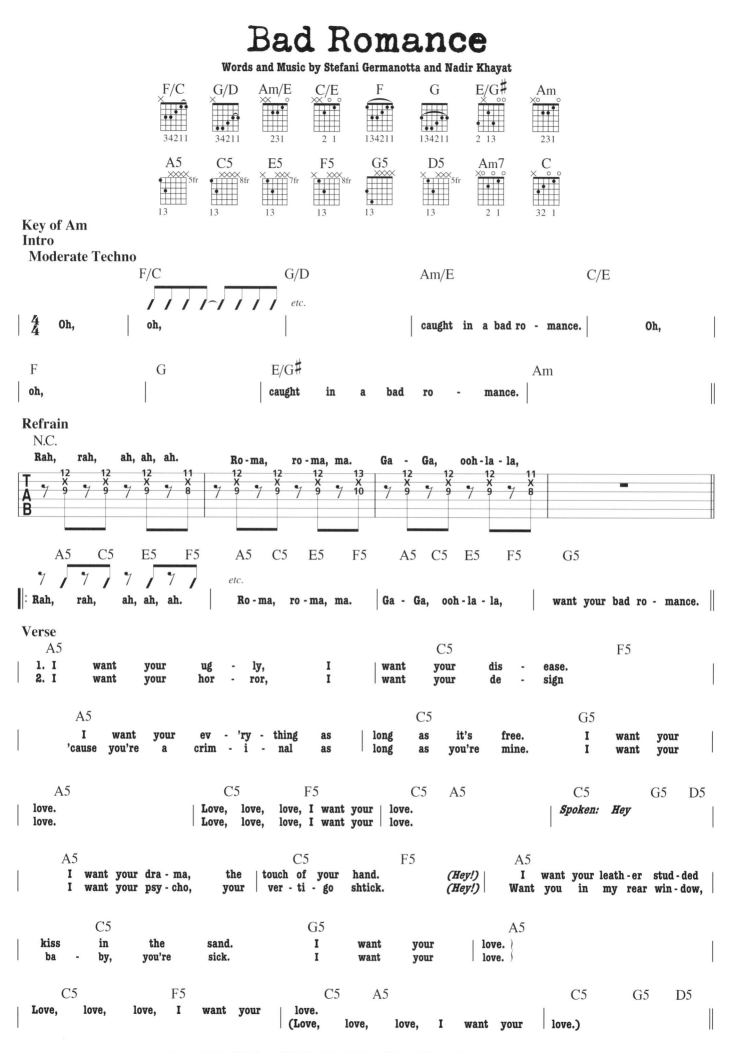

Pre-Chorus

Am7

Quiet, build to Chorus

etc.

You know that I want you, | *and you know that I need you.* | *I want it bad,*

※ Chorus
w/ Intro pattern

F | G

| bad ro - mance. ‖ I want your love and I | want your re - venge, you and me |

Am | C | F | G

| could write a bad ro - mance. | Oh, | I want your love and all your | lov - in's re - venge, you and me |

E/G♯ | Am | F | G | Am

| could write a bad ro - mance. | Oh, | oh, | | caught in a bad ro - mance. |

C | F | G | E/G♯ | Am | *To Coda* ⊕

| Oh, | oh, | | caught in a bad ro - mance. | ‖

Refrain

A5 C5 E5 F5 | A5 C5 E5 F5 | A5 C5 E5 F5 G5

‖: Rah, rah, ah, ah, ah. | Ro - ma, ro - ma, ma. | Ga - Ga, ooh - la - la, | want your bad ro - mance. :‖

Bridge

Am7
|1.

‖: Walk, walk, fash - ion ba - by. | Work it, move that bitch, c - ra - zy. | Walk, walk, fash - ion ba - by. |

|2.

| Work it, move that bitch, c - ra - zy. :‖ Walk, walk, pas - sion ba - by. | Work it, I'm a free bitch, ba - |

F | G | Am | C

| by. I want your love | and I want your re - venge. | I want your love, | I don't wan - na be friends. |

F | G | E/G♯ | Am

| Je ton a - mour, | et je veux ton re - venge. | Je ton a - mour. | I don't wan - na be friends. (Oh,

F | G | Am | C

| oh, | No, I don't wan - na be friends. | caught in a bad ro - mance. | I don't wan - na be friends. Oh,

F | G | E/G♯ | N.C. | *D.S. al Coda*

| oh, | Want your bad ro - mance. | caught in a bad ro - mance.) | Want your bad ro - mance. ‖

⊕ **Coda**

N.C.

| Rah, rah, ah, ah, ah. | Ro - ma, ro - ma, ma. | Ga - Ga, ooh - la - la, | want your bad ro - mance. ‖

Best of You

Words and Music by Dave Grohl, Taylor Hawkins, Chris Shiflett and Nate Mendel

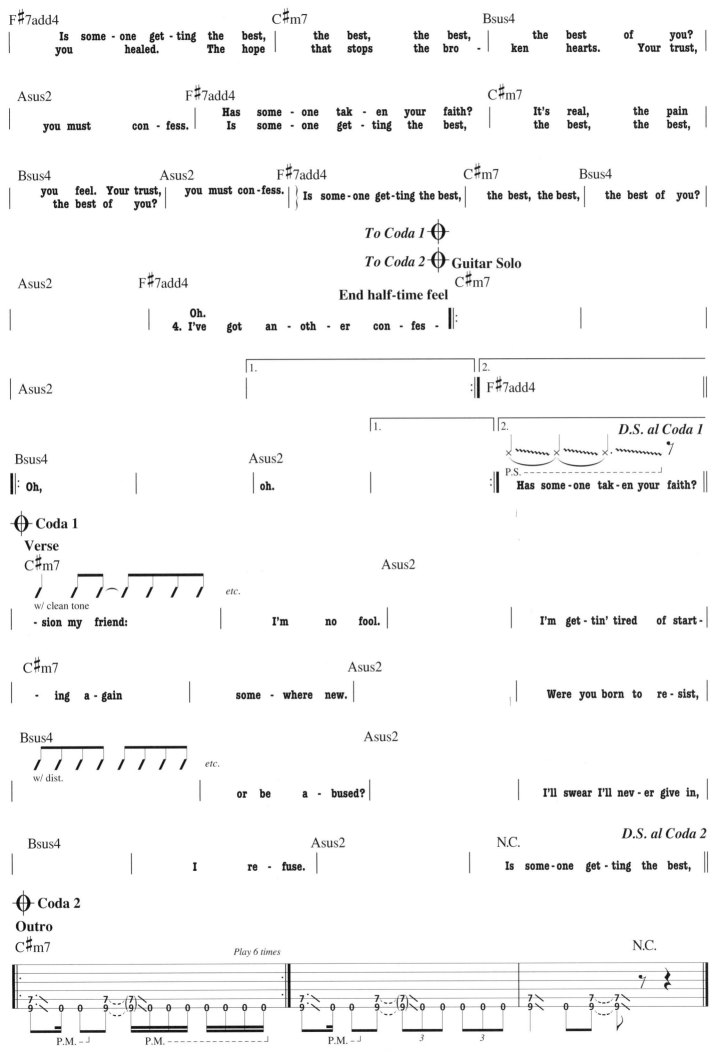

Black Horse and the Cherry Tree

Words and Music by Katie Tunstall

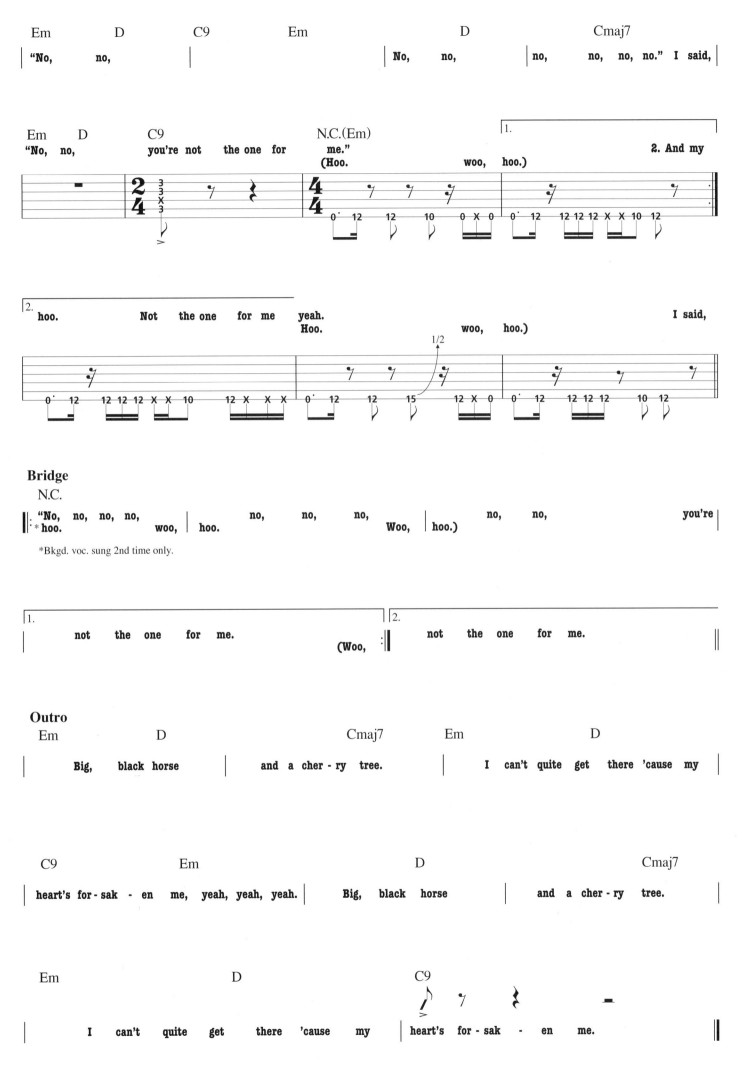

Bubbly

Words and Music by Colbie Caillat and Jason Reeves

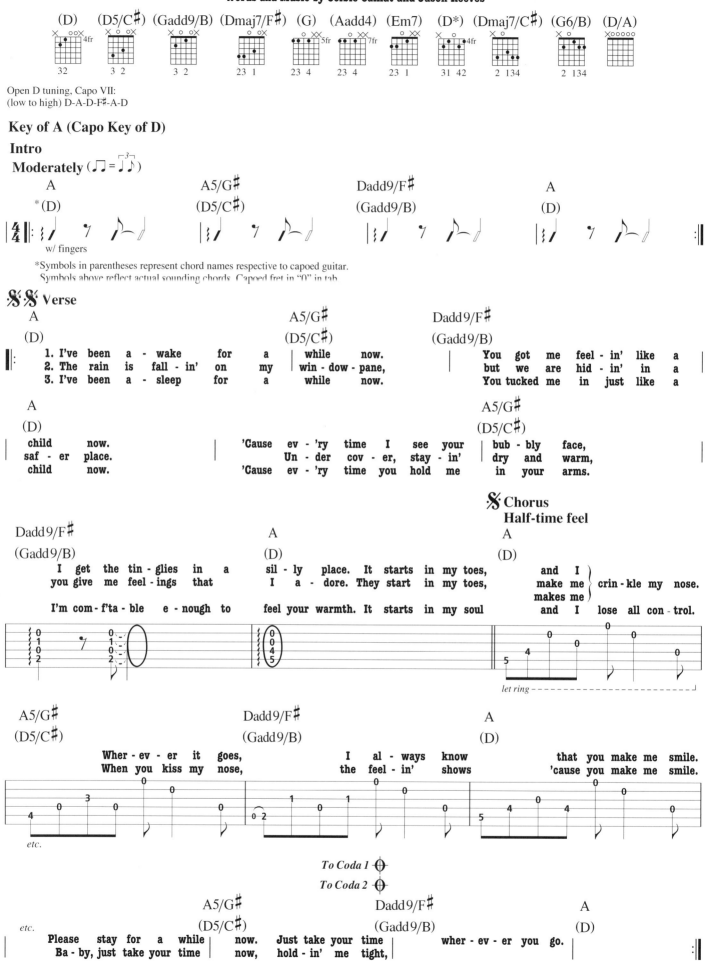

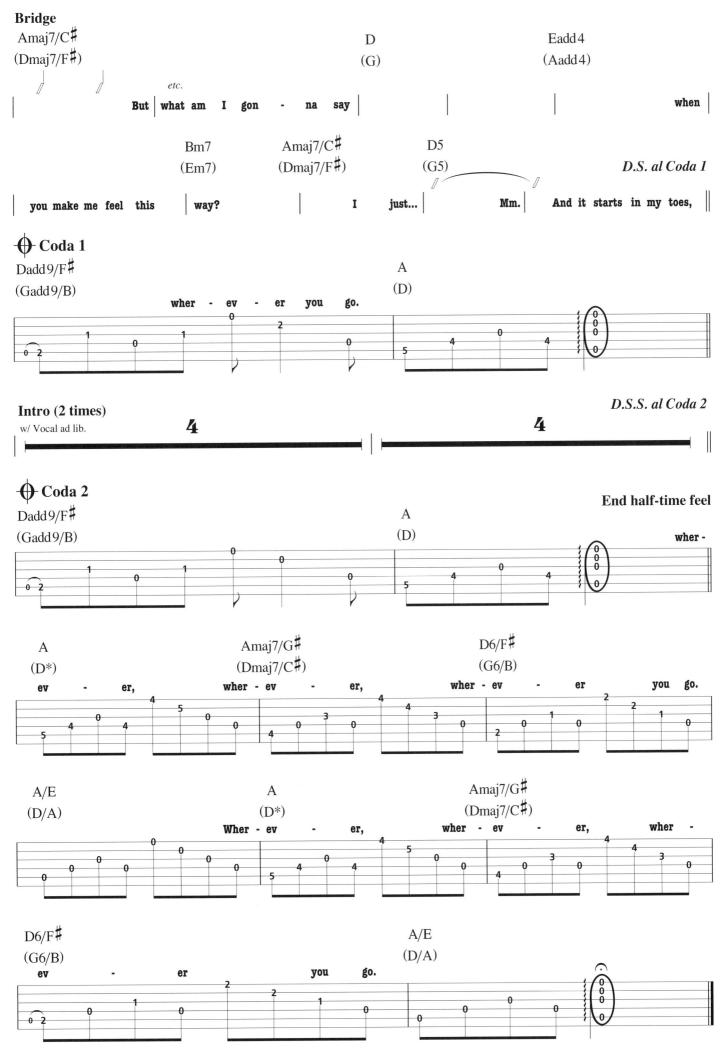

Bridge

Amaj7/C♯
(Dmaj7/F♯)

D
(G)

Eadd4
(Aadd4)

etc.

But what am I gon - na say when

Bm7
(Em7)

Amaj7/C♯
(Dmaj7/F♯)

D5
(G5)

D.S. al Coda 1

you make me feel this way? I just... Mm. And it starts in my toes,

Coda 1

Dadd9/F♯
(Gadd9/B)

A
(D)

wher - ev - er you go.

Intro (2 times)
w/ Vocal ad lib.

4

4

D.S.S. al Coda 2

Coda 2

Dadd9/F♯
(Gadd9/B)

A
(D)

End half-time feel

wher -

A
(D*)

Amaj7/G♯
(Dmaj7/C♯)

D6/F♯
(G6/B)

ev - er, wher - ev - er, wher - ev - er you go.

A/E
(D/A)

A
(D*)

Amaj7/G♯
(Dmaj7/C♯)

Wher - ev - er, wher - ev - er, wher -

D6/F♯
(G6/B)

A/E
(D/A)

ev - er you go.

Clocks

Words and Music by Guy Berryman, Jon Buckland, Will Champion and Chris Martin

Eb   Bbm   Fm   Gbmaj7   Db   Ab6   Gb

Key of Fm
Intro
Moderately

Eb   Bbm   Fm   *Play 4 times*

```
T  11      11      11      11   | 9                              | 8      8      8
A     11      12      12      11|    11      11      11   11      |    9      9      9
B  4                            |       10      10      10        |       10      10      9
   4                            |                        11   11  |
                                |                10      10       |
```

Piano arr. for gtr.
Band enters 3rd time

Verse

Eb   Bbm   Fm
1. Lights go out and I |can't be saved, |tides that I tried to swim |a - gainst have
2. Con - fu - sion (that) |nev - er stops (the) |clos - ing walls and |tick-ing clocks. Gon - na

Eb   Bbm   Fm
|brought me down up - |on my knees, |oh, I beg, I |beg and plead. Sing - ing:
|come back and |take you home. I |could not stop, that |you now know. Sing - ing:

Eb   Bbm   Fm
|come out of |things un - said, |shoot an ap - ple |off my head. And a
|come out up - |on my seas, |curse missed op - por - |tu - ni - ties. Am I

Eb   Bbm   Fm
|trou - ble that |can't be named, a |ti - ger's wait - ing |to be tamed. } Sing - ing:
|a part |of the cure, or |am I part of |the di - sease.

Chorus
2nd time, play Chorus 2 times

Eb   Bbm   Fm
| You | | | are. |

Eb   Bbm   Fm
| You | | | are. |

Interlude 1
w/ Intro riff

| Eb | | Bbm | | | | Fm | |

| Eb | | Bbm | | | | Fm | :||

Interlude 2

Eb   Bbm   Fm

```
16 15    16 15   16 15   16 15   16 15   16 15   16 15   16 15   16 15   16 15
   16        16        14        14        14        14        13        13
```

Chorus (1 time)   **Bridge**
w/ Interlude 2   Gbmaj7   Db   Ab6

8

Play 3 times

||: { 1., 3. And noth | - ing else | com - pares. | :||
{ 2. Oo,   oh,   noth | - ing else | com - pares.

| Gb | | Gbmaj7 | | Gb | | Gbmaj7 | ||

Intro (2 times)   **Interlude 2 (2 times)**   **Chorus (1 time)**
                                                      w/ Interlude 2

8   **8**   **8**

w/ Interlude 2
Eb   Bbm   Fm   *Play 4 times*

||: Home,   home, | where I | want - ed   to | go. :||

Outro   *Repeat and fade*
w/ Interlude 2

||: Eb | | Bbm | | | | Fm | :||

Come on Get Higher

Words and Music by Matt Nathanson and Mark Weinberg

(G/B)   (Csus2)   (G5)   (D)   (Em7)   (D/F#)

Capo II

Key of G (Capo Key of A)

Intro

Moderately slow

A/C#
*(G/B)   (Csus2)   (G5)

Dsus2   A5

*Symbols in parentheses represent chord names respective to capoed guitar.
Symbols above reflect actual sounding chords. Capoed fret is "0" in tab.

Verse

w/ Intro pattern

A/C#   Dsus2   A5   A/C#   Dsus2   A5
(G/B)   (Csus2)   (G5)   (G/B)   (Csus2)   (G5)

1. I miss the sound of your   voice,   and   I   miss the rush of your   skin.
2. I miss the sound of your   voice,   the loud - est   thing in   my   head.

A/C#   Dsus2   A5   A/C#   Dsus2   E
(G/B)   (Csus2)   (G5)   (G/B)   (Csus2)   (D)

And I miss the still of the si - lence   as you breathe out,   and I   breathe in.   } If I could
And I ache to re - mem - ber   all the vi - o - lent, sweet, per - fect   words   that you said.

Pre-Chorus

Dsus2   A5   F#m7   E
(Csus2)   (G5)   (Em7)   (D)

                                                                         1., 2. So,
walk on wa - ter, if I could tell you what's next,   I'd make you be - lieve,   I'd   make you for - get.

Chorus

Dsus2   A5   Dsus2   A5
(Csus2)   (G5)   (Csus2)   (G5)

come } on, get high - er. Loos - en my   lips.   Faith │ and de - sire   in the swing of your hips. Just
3. Come

Dsus2   A5   F#m7   E/G#
(Csus2)   (G5)   (Em7)   (D/F#)

pull   me   down   hard   and   drown │   me   in   love.   So,

Dsus2   A5   Dsus2   A5
(Csus2)   (G5)   (Csus2)   (G5)

come   on, get   high - er. Loos - en my   lips.   Faith │ and de - sire   in the swing of your hips. Just

To Coda ⊕ |1.

Dsus2	A5	F#m7	E/G#	F#m7	E
(Csus2)	(G5)	(Em7)	(D/F#)	(Em7)	(D)

|2.

| pull me down hard and drown | me in love. :‖ me in love. ‖

Bridge

Dsus2	F#m7	A5	E
(Csus2)	(Em7)	(G5)	(D)

| I miss the pull of your heart. | I taste the sparks on your tongue. | And I see an-gels and dev - | ils and God when you come |

Dsus2	F#m7	E	E/G#
(Csus2)	(Em7)	(D)	(D/F#)

| on. Hold | on, hold on, | hold on, hold | on love. ‖

Interlude

A/C#	Dsus2	A5	A/C#	Dsus2	A5
(G/B)	(Csus2)	(G5)	(G/B)	(Csus2)	(G5)

| Sing sha, | la, la, la. | Sing sha, | la, la, la, la. Hoo, |

D.S. al Coda

A/C#	Dsus2	A5	A/C#	Dsus2	E
(G/B)	(Csus2)	(G5)	(G/B)	(Csus2)	(D)

| hoo. | Hoo, | oo, hoo, hoo, | oo. ‖

⊕ **Coda**

Outro

F#m7	E/G#	Dsus2	A5	Dsus2	A5
(Em7)	(D/F#)	(Csus2)	(G5)	(Csus2)	(G5)

| me, drown me in love. | It's all wrong. | It's all wrong. |
(Come on, get high - er. Loos - en my lips. Faith | and de - sire in the swing of your hips.

Dsus2	A5	F#m7	E/G#
(Csus2)	(G5)	(Em7)	(D/F#)

| It's all | right. So, come on, |
| Pull me down hard and drown | me in love. So |

Dsus2	A5	Dsus2	A5
(Csus2)	(G5)	(Csus2)	(G5)

| get high - er. Come on, | get high - er. 'Cause ev - |
come on, get high - er. Loos - en my lips. Faith | and de - sire in the swing of your hips. Just |

Dsus2	A5	F#m7	E/G#	Dsus2
(Csus2)	(G5)	(Em7)	(D/F#)	(Csus2)

| 'ry - thing works, 'cause ev - | 'ry - thing works in your | arms. ‖
pull me down hard.)

Crazy

Words and Music by Brian Burton, Thomas Callaway, GianPiero Reverberi and GianFranco Reverberi

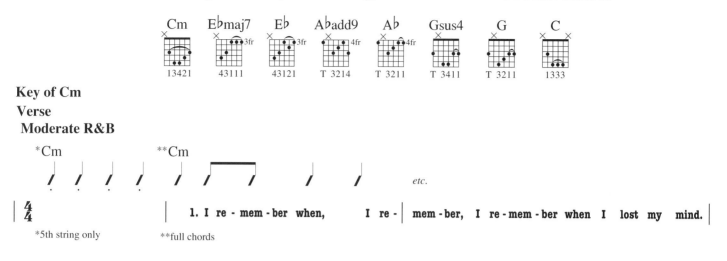

Key of Cm
Verse
Moderate R&B

*Cm   **Cm   etc.

4/4

*5th string only   **full chords

1. I re - mem - ber when,   I re - | mem - ber, I re - mem - ber when I lost my mind.

E♭maj7

There was | some - thing so pleas - ant a - bout that place.

E♭

A♭add9

E - ven your e - mo - tions have an

A♭

ech - o   in so much   space. |

Gsus4

G

Mm. |

Verse
Cm

2. And when you're out   there   with - out a | care,   yeah, I   was   out   of   touch,
3. Come on   now,   who do you,   who do | you, who do you, who do you think you are?
4. ev - er since   I was lit - tle,   ev - er | since   I was lit - tle   it looked   like   fun.

E♭maj7

E♭

A♭add9

but it | was - n't be - cause I did - n't know e - nough.
        Ha,   ha,   ha,   bless   your   soul.
And it's   no   co - in - ci - dence I've come

A♭			Gsus4		G		* N.C.	

	I just knew too much.			Mm,	does that make me cra-
You real-ly think you're in con-trol?				*Well,*	I think you're cra-
and I can die when I'm done.				But, may-be I'm cra-

Chorus

Cm			E♭maj7			E♭	

- zy?	Does that make me cra - zy?		Does that make me cra-
- zy.	I think you're cra - zy.		I think you're cra-
- zy.	May - be you're cra - zy.		May - be we're cra-

A♭add9		A♭		Gsus4		G	

- zy?	Pos - si - bly.
- zy	just like me.
- zy,	prob - a - bly.

Bridge

C							A♭add9	

And I hope that you are hav- in' the time of your	life,	
My he-roes had the heart to lose their lives out on the limb.	
Mm,	oo,

A♭			E♭maj7					

| but think twice. | That's my on - ly ad - vice, |
| And all I re - mem- ber is think- in', I wan - na be like them. |
| mm, | woo, |

Gsus4		G		Cm	

Play 3 times

| | | mm. |
| Mm. |
| mm. |

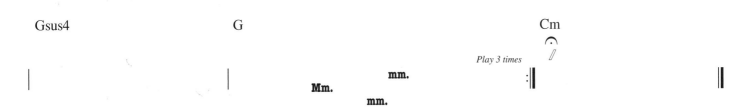

Drops of Jupiter

(Tell Me)

Words and Music by Pat Monahan, Jimmy Stafford, Rob Hotchkiss, Charlie Colin and Scott Underwood

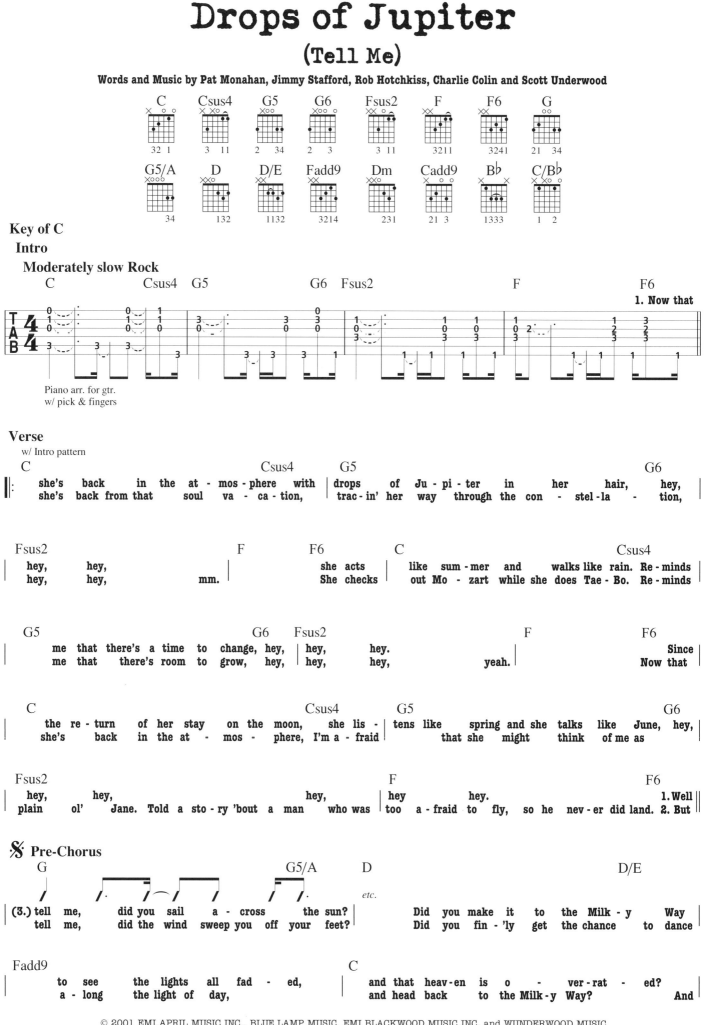

Key of C

Intro

Moderately slow Rock

Piano arr. for gtr.
w/ pick & fingers

Verse

w/ Intro pattern

C she's back in the at-mos-phere with **Csus4** drops of Ju-pi-ter in her hair, hey, **G5** **G6**
she's back from that soul va-ca-tion, trac-in' her way through the con-stel-la-tion,

Fsus2 hey, hey, **F** **F6** she acts **C** like sum-mer and walks like rain. Re-minds **Csus4**
hey, hey, mm. She checks out Mo-zart while she does Tae-Bo. Re-minds

G5 me that there's a time to change, hey, **G6 Fsus2** hey, hey. **F** **F6** Since
me that there's room to grow, hey, hey, hey, yeah. Now that

C the re-turn of her stay on the moon, she lis- **Csus4** tens like spring and she talks like June, hey, **G5** **G6**
she's back in the at-mos-phere, I'm a-fraid that she might think of me as

Fsus2 hey, hey, **F** hey, hey hey. **F6** 1.Well
plain ol' Jane. Told a sto-ry 'bout a man who was too a-fraid to fly, so he nev-er did land. 2.But

Pre-Chorus

G (3.) tell me, did you sail a-cross the sun? **G5/A D** Did you make it to the Milk-y **D/E** Way
tell me, did the wind sweep you off your feet? Did you fin-'ly get the chance to dance

Fadd9 to see the lights all fad-ed, **C** and that heav-en is o-ver-rat-ed? And
a-long the light of day, and head back to the Milk-y Way?

G			G5/A	D		

Tell me,   did you fall   from a shoot-ing star,   one   with-out   a   per-ma-nent
tell me,   did Ve-nus   blow your | mind?   Was it   ev-'ry-thing you want-ed   to   find?

Dm				Fadd9		

scar, } and did   you miss   me   while   you were | look-in'   for { 1., 2. your-self   out   there? ||
                                                             3. your-self?

1.

Interlude
w/ Intro pattern

C		Csus4	G5		G6	Fsus2		F		F6

2. Now that

2.

Chorus

Cadd9						G6					

* (Na,   na,   na,   na,   na,   na, | na   na,   na,   na,   na,   na,
*Bkgd. voc. sung 2nd & 3rd times only.

Fsus2								

       2. And did you fin-'ly get the chance to dance | a - long   the light of   day?
na,   na.

Cadd9						G6					

love,   pride,   deep   -   fried   chick - en,   your | best   friend   al   -   ways   stick - in'
                                                           And did you
Na,   na,   na,   na,   na,   na,   na,   na,   na,   na,   na,   na,

Fsus2								

up   for   you   from a shoot-ing star, | e - ven when I know you're   wrong? Can you im - ag - ine no
fall   from a shoot-ing   star, | fall   from a   shoot-ing   star?
na,   na.

Cadd9						G6					

first   dance,   freeze   -   dried   ro - mance, | five   hour   phone con - ver - sa   -   tion,   the
                                                            And are you
Na,   na,   na,   na,   na,   na,   na,   na,   na,   na,   na,   na,

B♭		C/B♭		B♭				F		*Fine*

best   soy   lat - te that   you   ev - er   had   and | me?   But
lone - ly   look-in' for   your - self   out   there? | ||
na,   na.)

Pre-Chorus

G					G5/A	D				D/E

tell   me,   did the wind sweep you   off   your feet? | Did   you   fin - 'ly   get   the chance   to   dance |

D.S. al Fine
(take 2nd ending)

Fadd9					C				

    a - long   the light of   day, | and head   back   to   the Milk - y Way?   And ||

Fireflies

Words and Music by Adam Young

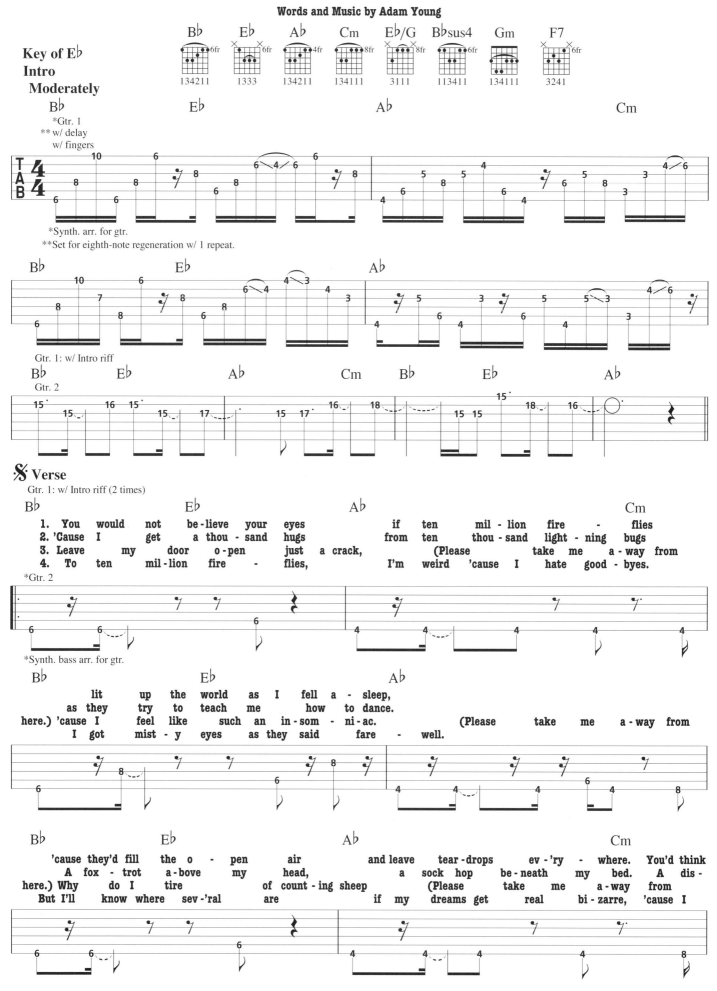

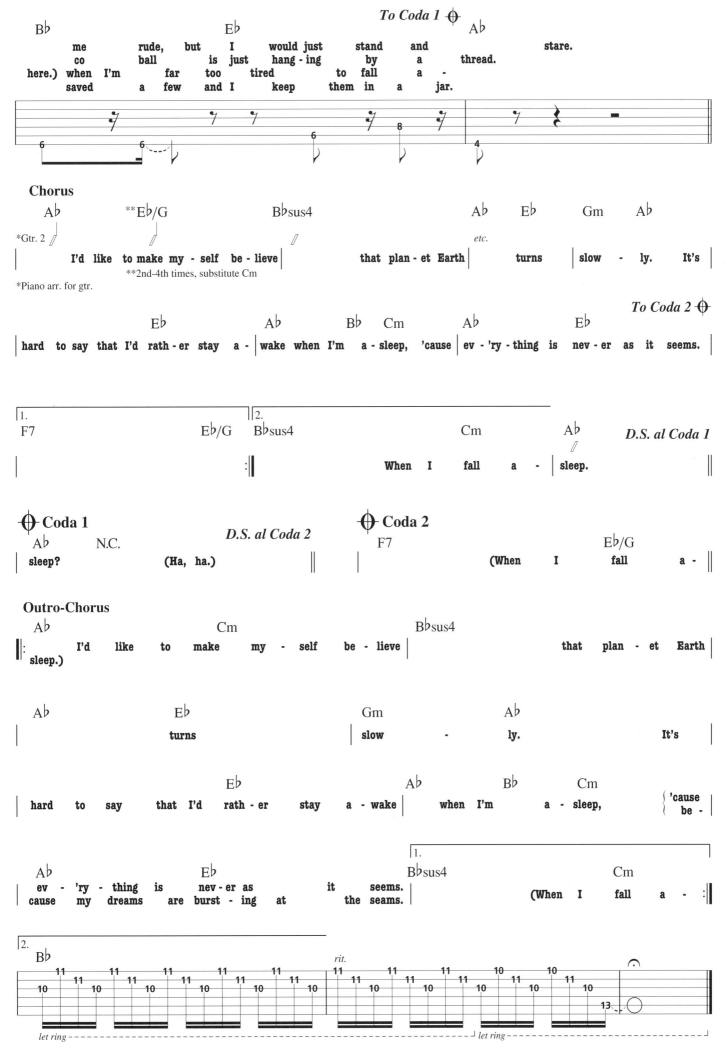

Gives You Hell

Words and Music by Tyson Ritter and Nick Wheeler

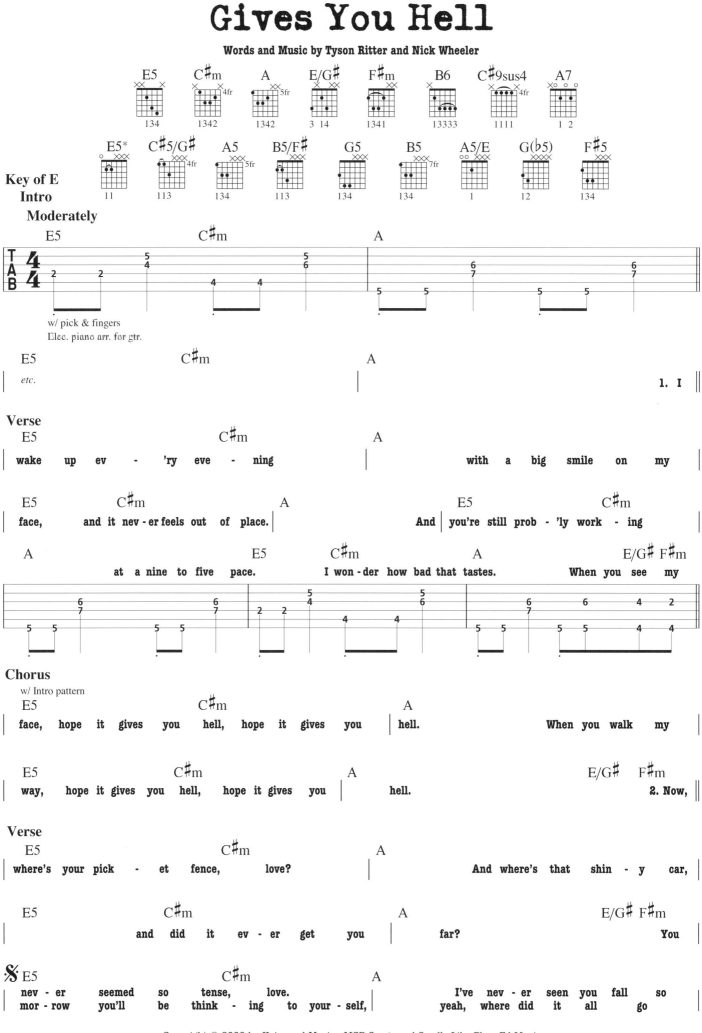

Key of E
Intro
Moderately

w/ pick & fingers
Elec. piano arr. for gtr.

etc.

1. I

Verse

wake up ev - 'ry eve - ning

with a big smile on my

face, and it nev - er feels out of place.

And you're still prob - 'ly work - ing

at a nine to five pace. I won - der how bad that tastes.

When you see my

Chorus
w/ Intro pattern

face, hope it gives you hell, hope it gives you

hell.

When you walk my

way, hope it gives you hell, hope it gives you

hell.

2. Now,

Verse

where's your pick - et fence, love?

And where's that shin - y car,

and did it ev - er get you

far?

You

nev - er seemed so tense, love.
mor - row you'll be think - ing to your - self,

I've nev - er seen you fall so
yeah, where did it all go

E5   C♯m   A

hard.   And   do   you   know   where   you   are?   And

wrong?   But   the   list   goes   on   and   on.   (And   the

Pre-Chorus

B6   C♯9sus4   B6   A7

truth   be   told,   I   miss   you.   And   truth   be   told,   I'm   ly - ing.   When   you   see   my

truth   be   told,   I   miss   you.   Truth,   I'm   ly - ing.)

let ring   *let ring*   *let ring*

Chorus

E5*   C♯5/G♯   A5

face, hope   it   gives   you   hell, hope   it   gives   you   hell.   When   you   walk   my

E5*   C♯5/G♯   A5   E5*   C♯5/G♯

way, hope   it   gives   you   hell, hope   it   gives   you   hell.   If   you   find   a   man   that's   worth   a   damn   and   treats   you

A5   E5*   B5/F♯   *To Coda* ⊕   A5   G5

well,   then   he's   a   fool.   You're   just   as   well, hope   it   gives   you   hell.   I   hope   it   gives   you

Interlude

w/ Intro pattern

E5   C♯m   A   E5   C♯m   A   *D.S. al Coda*

hell.   3. To -

⊕ Coda

A5   B5   C♯5/G♯   A5/E

Bridge

hell.   Now,   you'll   nev - er   see   what   you've   done   to   me.   You   can

E5*   E/G♯   B/F♯   E5*   C♯5/G♯

take   back   your   mem - o - ries, they're   no   good   to   me.   And   here's   to   all   your   lies,   you   can

G(♭5)   F♯5   B5/F♯

look   me   in   the   eyes   with   the   sad,   sad   look   that   you   wear   so   well.

Outro-Chorus

1st time, bass & drums only.
2nd time, w/ band.

E5*   A5

Gang vocals: When   you   see   my ‖: face, hope   it   gives   you   hell,   hope   it   gives   you   hell.   When   you   walk   my

                                                   * **(Hope it gives you hell!)**

*Background vocals sung 2nd time only.

C♯5/G♯   B5/F♯   E5*

way,   hope   it   gives   you   hell, hope   it   gives   you   hell.   When   you   find   a   man   that's   worth   a   damn   and   treats   you

                                               When   you   hear   this   song   and   you   sing   a - long   but   you   nev-er tell,

                                       Hope   it   gives   you   hell!

A5   C♯5/G♯   B5/F♯   E5*   C♯5/G♯   B5/F♯

well,   then   he's   a   fool.   You're   just   as   well, hope   it   gives   you   hell. When   you   see   my   song,   I   hope   that   it   will   give   you

       then   you're   the   fool.   I'm   just   as   well, hope   it   gives   you   hell. When   you   hear   this

But   you   nev-er tell.   Hope   it   gives   you   hell!

E5*   C♯5/G♯   B5/F♯   E5

hell.   You   can   sing   a - long,   I   hope   that   it   puts   you   through   hell.

Hope   it   gives   you   hell!)

Heaven

Words and Music by Henry Garza, Joey Garza and Ringo Garza

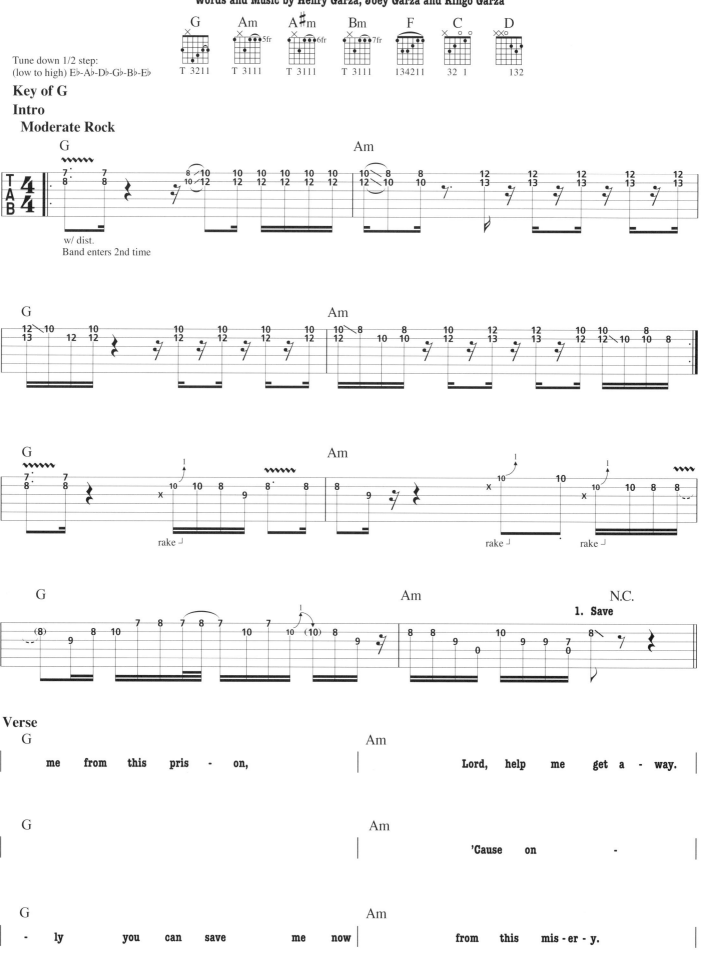

Tune down 1/2 step:
(low to high) Eb-Ab-Db-Gb-Bb-Eb

Key of G
Intro
Moderate Rock

w/ dist.
Band enters 2nd time

Verse

G   Am
me from this pris - on,   Lord, help me get a - way.

G   Am
                                                         'Cause on -

G   Am
- ly you can save me now   from this mis - er - y.

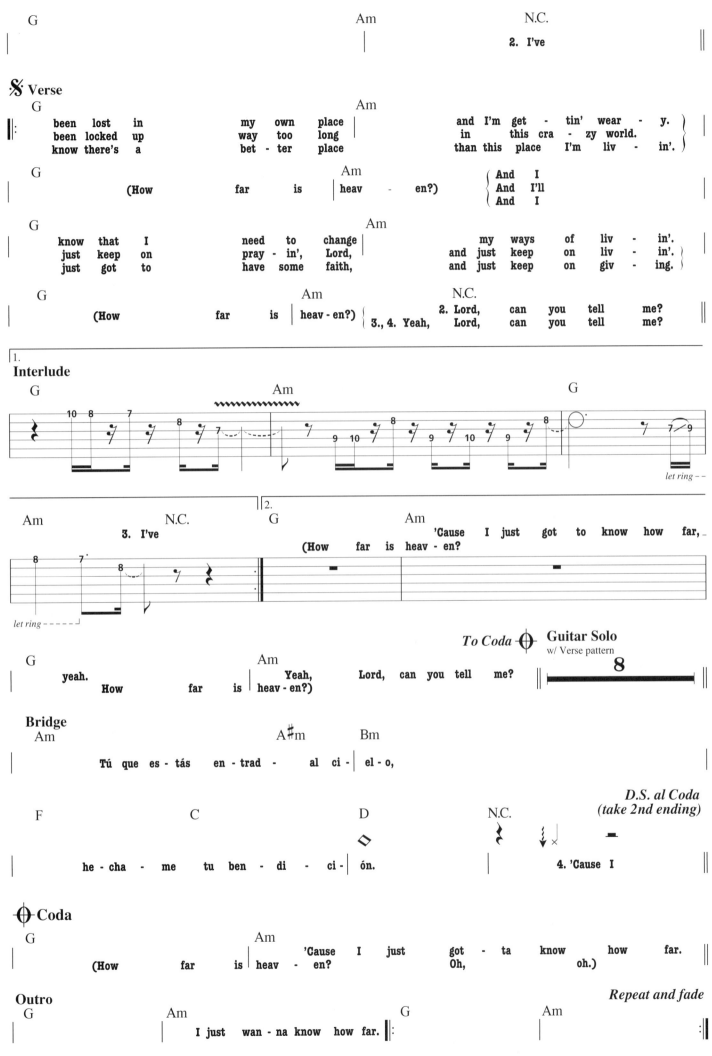

Hero of War

Words and Music by Joseph Principe, Timothy McIlrath, Brandon Barnes and Zach Blair

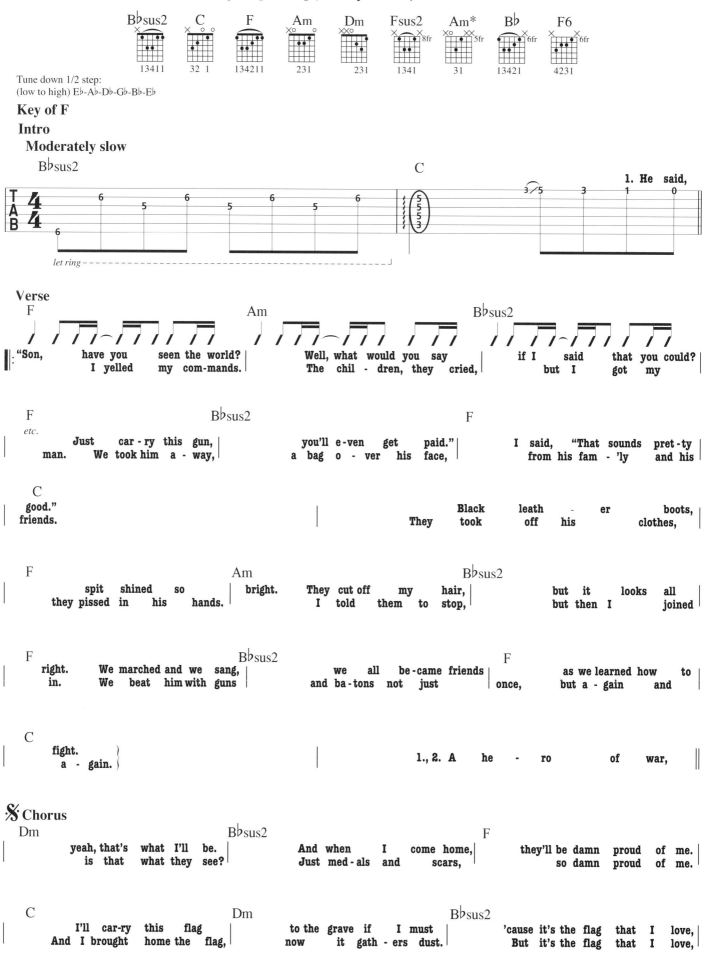

Hey, Soul Sister

Words and Music by Pat Monahan, Espen Lind and Amund Bjorkland

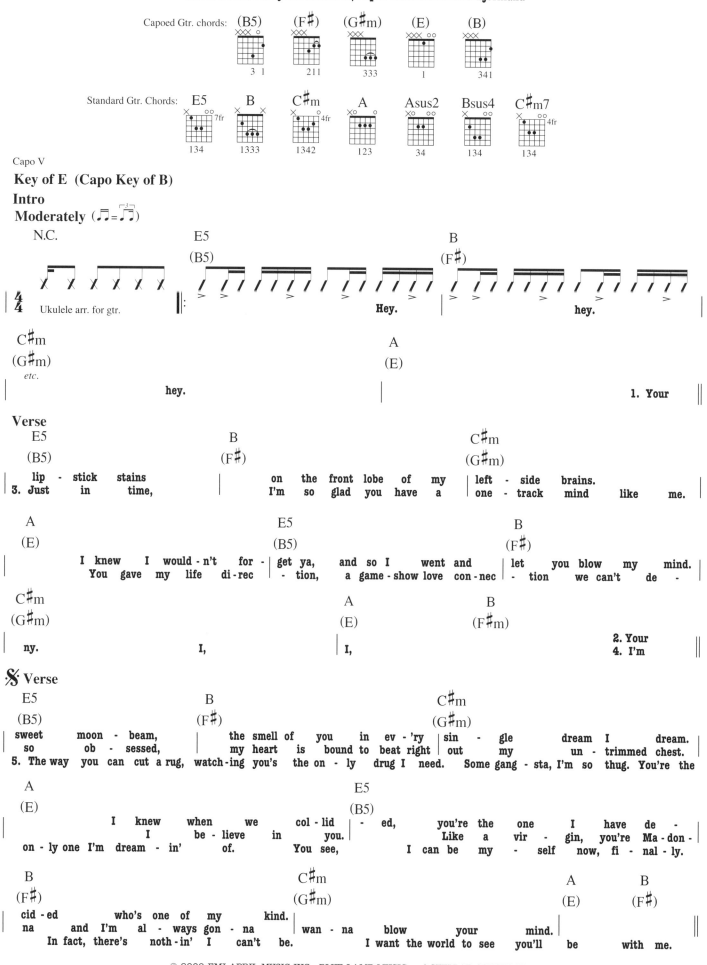

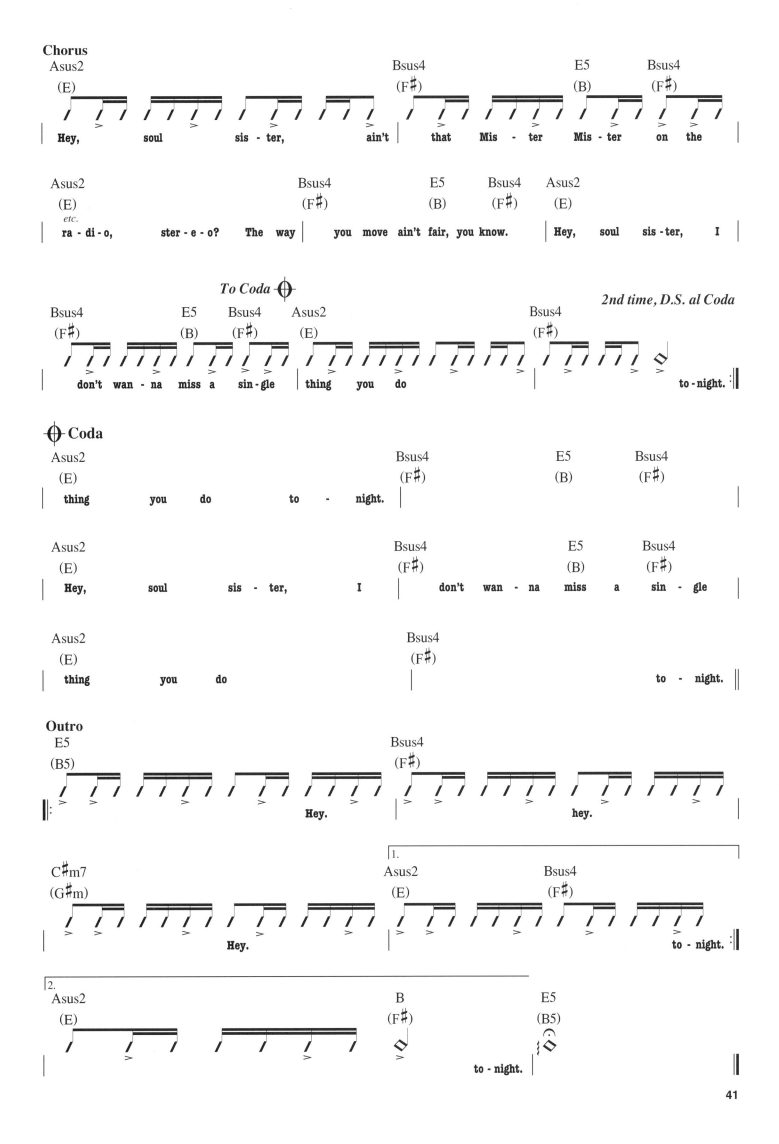

How to Save a Life

Words and Music by Joseph King and Isaac Slade

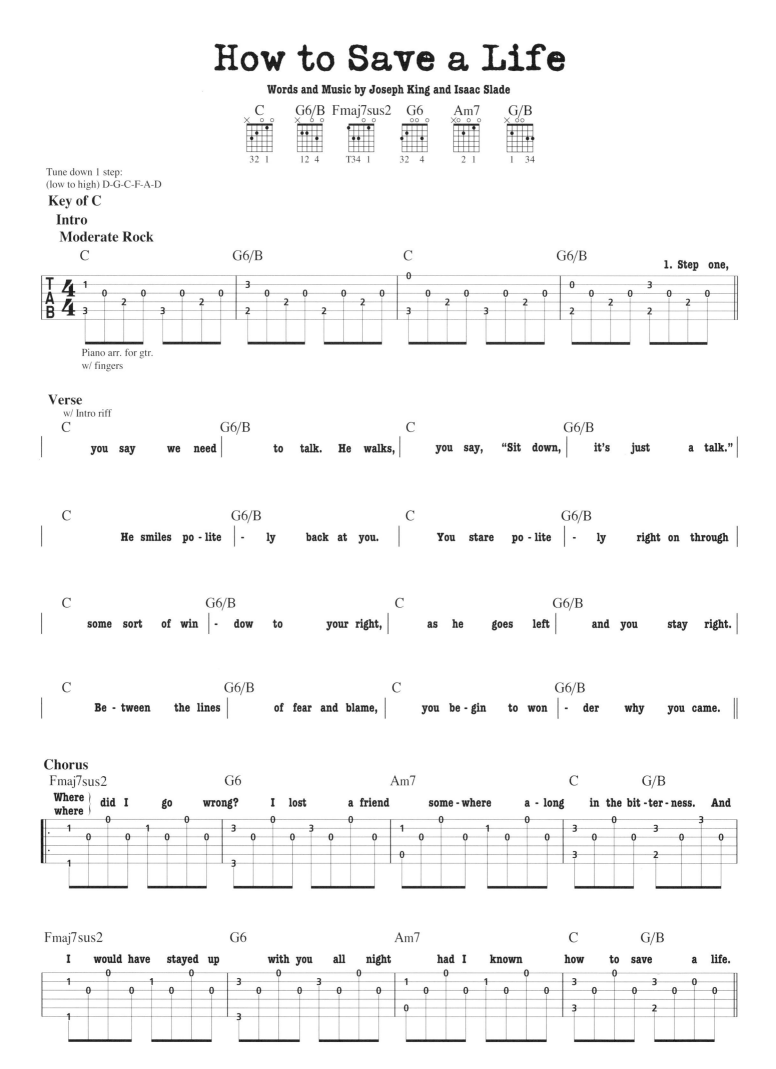

Interlude
w/ Intro riff

C	G6/B	*C	G6/B	

*2nd time, substitute Am7

Verse
w/ Intro riff

C .... **G6/B** **Am7**

2. Let him know that you know best, 'cause | af - ter all you do
he be - gins to raise | know his voice, you low - er yours and grant

G6/B .... **C** **G6/B**

know best. last choice. | de - fense or
him one last choice. Drive un - til you lose | the road or

Am7 .... **G6/B** .... **C**

with - out grant - ing in - | no - cence. Lay down a list
break with the ones you've fol - | lowed. He will do one

G6/B .... **Am7** **G6/B**

of what is wrong: | the things you've told | him all a - long. And
of two things: He will ad - mit to ev | - 'ry - thing,

C .... **G6/B** .... **Am7** **G6/B**

pray to God he hears | you, and | pray to God he hears | you. And
or he'll say he's just | not the same and | you'll be - gin to won - | der why you came.

Chorus (2 times)

|: **16** :|

Interlude
w/ Intro riff

3 .... **G6/B**

How to save a life.

C .... **G6/B** .... **C** **G6/B**

How to save a life.

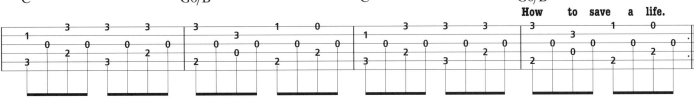

Outro
w/ Intro riff

4 .... **C**

I Gotta Feeling

Words and Music by Will Adams, Allan Pineda, Jaime Gomez, Stacy Ferguson, David Guetta and Frederic Riesterer

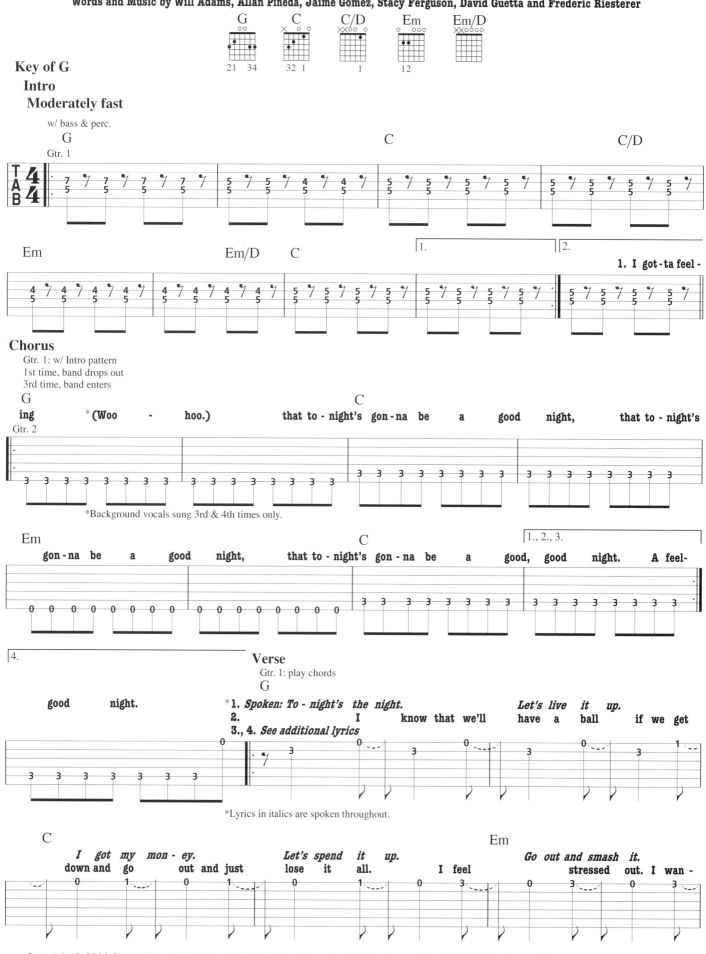

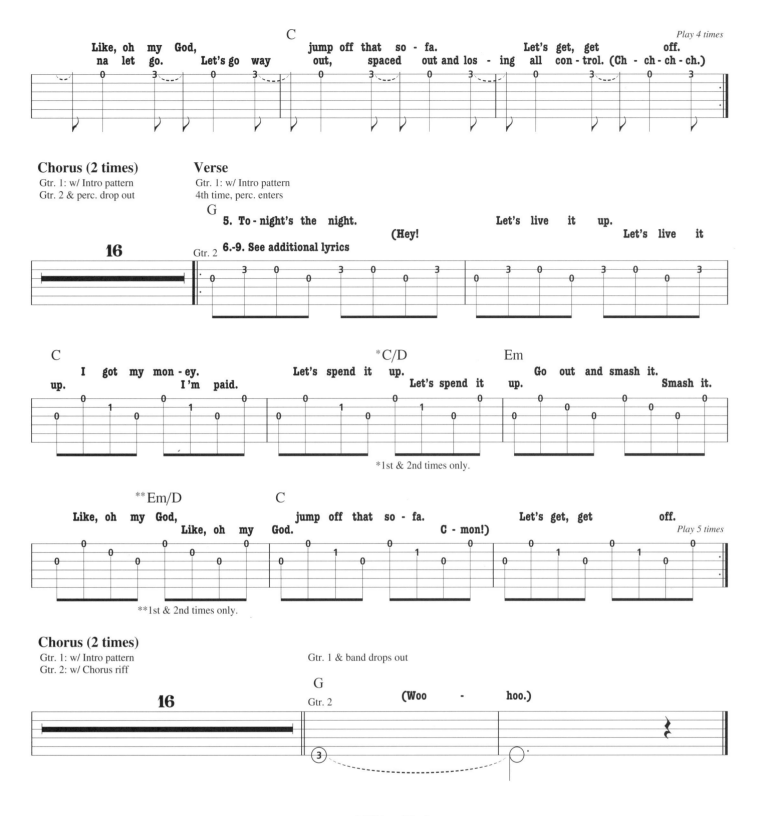

Additional Lyrics

3. Fill up my cup. Mazel tov!
Look at her dancing; just take it off.
Let's paint the town. We'll shut it down.
Let's burn the roof and then we'll do it again.

4. Let's do it, let's do it, let's do it, let's do it,
And do it, and do it, let's live it up and do it,
And do it, and do it, do it, do it.
Let's do it. Let's do it. Let's do it, 'cause I gotta feeling...

6. Fill up my cup. (Drink!) Mazel tov! (L'chayim!)
Look at her dancing; (Move it, move it.) just take it off.
Let's paint the town. (Paint the town.)
We'll shut it down. (We'll shut it down.)
Let's burn the roof (Woo.) and then we'll do it again.

7. Let's do it, let's do it, let's do it, let's do it,
And do it, and do it, let's live it up and do it,
And do it, and do it, do it, do it.
Let's do it. Let's do it. Let's do it, do it, do it, do it.

8. Here we come, here we go. We gotta rock.
Easy come, easy go. Now we on top.
Feel the shot, body rock. Rock it, don't stop.
'Round and 'round, up and down, around the clock.

9. Monday, Tuesday, Wednesday and Thursday. (Do it!)
Friday, Saturday. Saturday to Sunday (Do it.)
Get, get, get, get, get with us. You know what we say, say:
Party ev'ry day. P-P-P-Party ev'ry day. And I'm feeling...

If You Only Knew

Words and Music by Brent Smith and Dave Bassett

Am   Fmaj7   C   Dm   G   G6/B   Am7   F

231   T3421   32 1 231   32 4   2   2 1   134211

Key of Am

Intro

Moderately

N.C.

(Synth & gtr.)   *

```
T  4           5/(9)      (9)   10/12    (7)      (7).   7      (4)      (4)   5   7
A  4  -
B  4
```

*Strum as fast as possible.

Verse

Am

1. If you on - ly knew   I'm hang - in' by a thread. The
2. If you on - ly knew   how man - y times I count - ed

Fmaj7   C   Fmaj7   C

web   I   spin   for   you.
all   the words   that   went   wrong.

Am   Fmaj7   C   Fmaj7   C

If you on - ly knew   I'd sac - ri - fice my beat - ing   heart be - fore   I lose   you.
If you on - ly knew   how I re - fuse to let you   go   e - ven when you're   gone.

𝄋 **Pre-Chorus**

Dm

I   still   hold   on   to   the   let - ters
I   don't   re - gret   an - y   days   I   spent,
I   still   hold   on   to   the   let - ters

G

you   re - turned.   I   swear,   I've   lived   and   learned.
nights   we   shared   or   let - ters   that   I   sent.
you   re - turned.   You   helped   me   live   and   learn.

**C   G6/B   Am7   G

It's four - o - three   and I   can't sleep.   With - out you next to me, I   toss and turn like the sea.

**3rd time, let chords ring, next 3 meas.

C	G6/B	Am7	G
If I drown to-night,	bring me back to life.	Breathe your breath in me. The	on-ly thing that I still be-

F	C	G	Am		F	C	G
lieve in is			you.	If	you on - ly knew.		

1.

Am		Fmaj7 C	Fmaj7 C

2.

Am	F	C	G
	If	you on - ly knew.		

Interlude

Am

1.

Fmaj7 C | Fmaj7 C

2. *D.S. al Coda*

Fmaj7 C

⊕ **Coda**
Outro

C	G6/B	Am7
lieve in is you.		Be - lieve in is you.
(If I drown to - night,	bring me back to life.	If I drown to - night,

G	F	C	G	Am
I still be -	lieve in you.			
bring me back to life.	You on - ly	knew.		If

F	C	G	Am
Oh, oh, oh.			If you on - ly knew.
you on - ly knew.)			

It's Not My Time

Words by Brad Arnold
Music by Brad Arnold, Robert Harrell, Christopher Henderson and Matthew Roberts

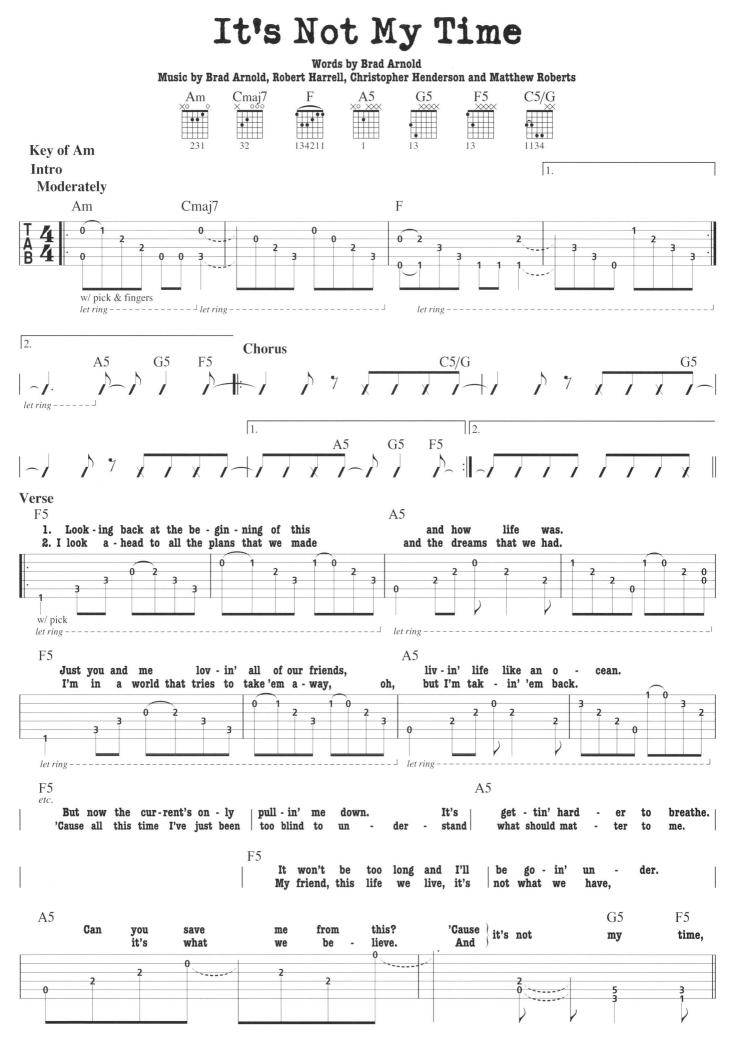

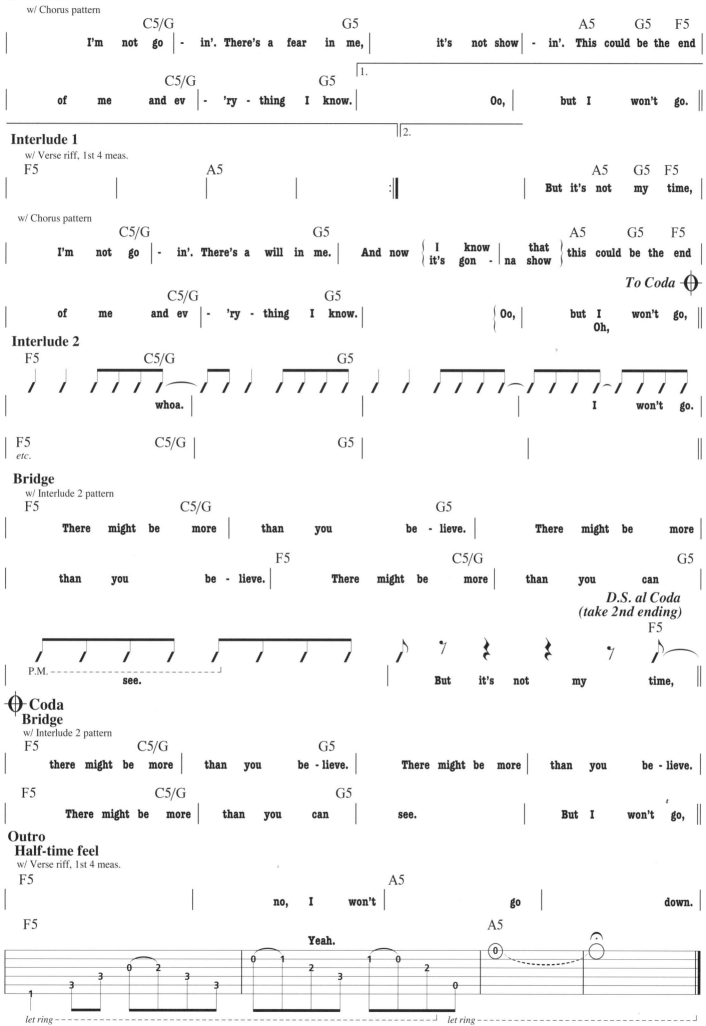

Just the Way You Are

Words and Music by Bruno Mars, Ari Levine, Philip Lawrence, Khari Cain and Khalil Walton

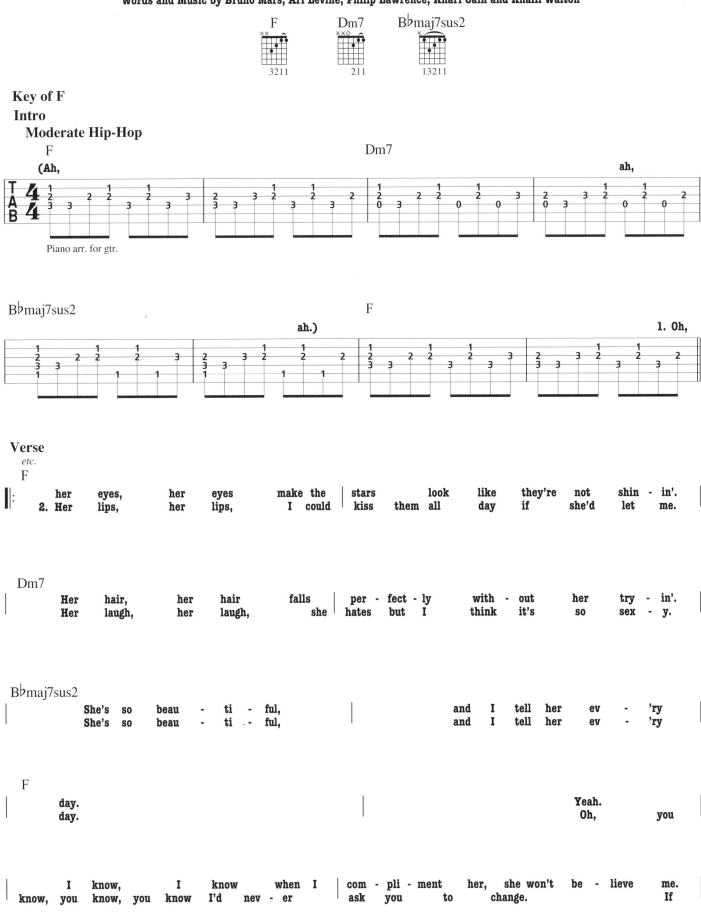

Dm7

And it's so, it's so sad to | think that she don't see what I see.
per - fect's what you're search - in' for then | just stay the same. So

B♭maj7sus2 .... **F**

But ev -'ry time she asks me, "Do | I look o - kay?" I say: |
don't e - ven both - er ask - in' if | you look o - kay. You know I'll | say:

𝄋 **Chorus**

F **Dm7**

When I see your face, ‖ | there's not a thing | that I would change,

B♭maj7sus2

'cause you're a - maz | - ing just | the way you are.

F

| And when you smile, |

Dm7

the whole world stops | and stares for a while, | 'cause, girl, you're a - maz -

To Coda ⊕ .... 1.

B♭maj7sus2 .... **F**

- ing just | the way you are. | | Yeah. :‖

2. .... **Bridge**

F

The way you are, ‖ | the way you are.

Dm7 .... **B♭maj7sus2**

| Girl, you're a - maz | - ing just |

D.S. al Coda

F

the way you are. | | When I see your face, ‖

⊕ **Coda**

w/ Intro riff, 1st 2 meas.
F

| | Yeah. 𝄂

Life After You

Words and Music by Chris Daughtry, Brett James, Chad Kroeger and Joey Moi

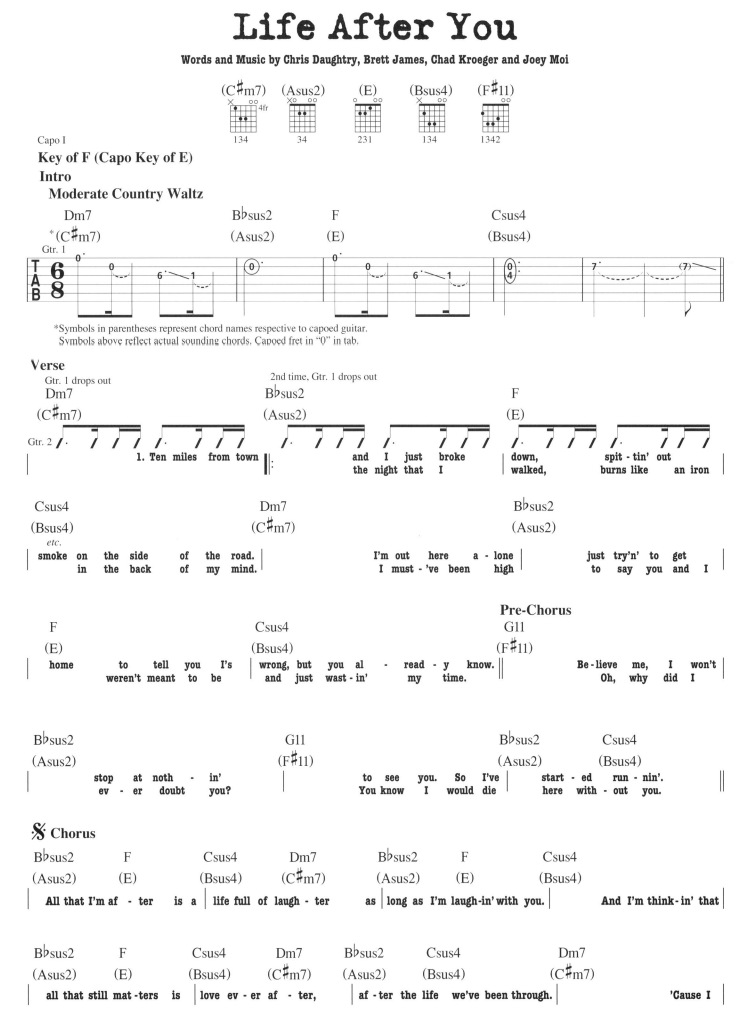

To Coda ⊕

[1.]

B♭sus2	Csus4	Dm7	B♭sus2	F
(Asus2)	(Bsus4)	(C♯m7)	(Asus2)	(E)

know there's no life af-ter you. Gtr. 1

[2.]

Csus4	Verse Dm7	Bridge Dm7
(Bsus4)	(C♯m7)	(C♯m7)

2. The last time we talked, You and I, right or wrong,

B♭sus2	F	Csus4	Dm7
(Asus2)	(E)	(Bsus4)	(C♯m7)

there's no oth-er one. Af-ter this time spent a-lone, it's hard to be-lieve that a man with sight could be so blind.

B♭sus2	F	Csus4
(Asus2)	(E)	(Bsus4)

Think-in' 'bout the bet-ter times, must-'ve been out of my mind. So I'm run-nin' back to tell you:

Chorus

B♭sus2	F	Csus4	Dm7
(Asus2)	(E)	(Bsus4)	(C♯m7)

All that I'm af-ter is a life full of laugh-ter. With-

Gtr. 2

B♭sus2	F	Csus4
(Asus2)	(E)	(Bsus4)

out you, God knows what I'd do, yeah.

D.S. al Coda

⊕ **Coda**

Outro

[1., 2., 3.]

B♭sus2	F	Csus4
(Asus2)	(E)	(Bsus4)

[4.]

Csus4	F
(Bsus4)	(E)

‖: Know there's no life af-ter you, know there's no life af-ter you. :‖ yeah. ◆

Lips of an Angel

Words and Music by Austin Winkler, Ross Hanson, Lloyd Garvey, Mark King, Michael Rodden and Brian Howes

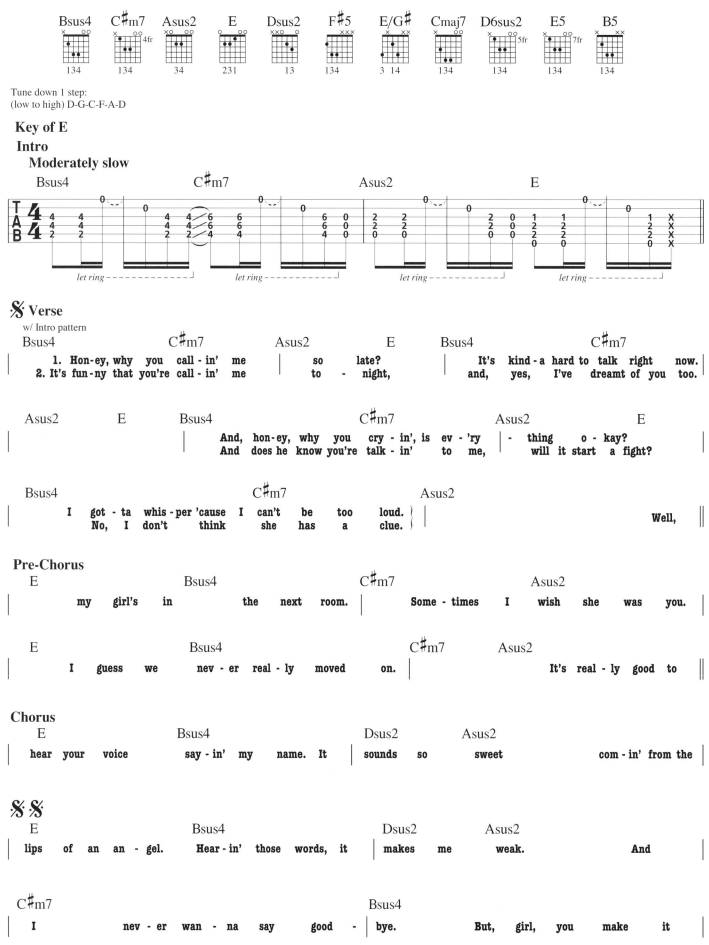

© 2005 EMI BLACKWOOD MUSIC INC., HINDER MUSIC CO. and HIGH BUCK PUBLISHING
All Rights Controlled and Administered by EMI BLACKWOOD MUSIC INC.
All Rights Reserved   International Copyright Secured   Used by Permission

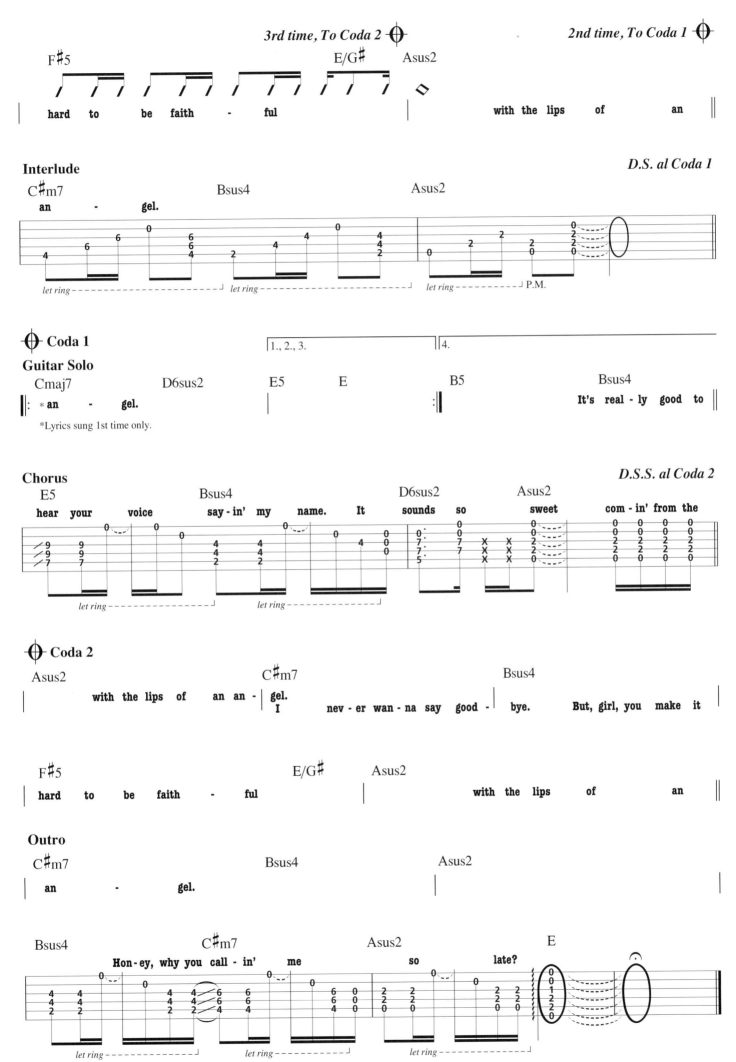

Lucky

Words and Music by Jason Mraz, Colbie Caillat and Timothy Fagan

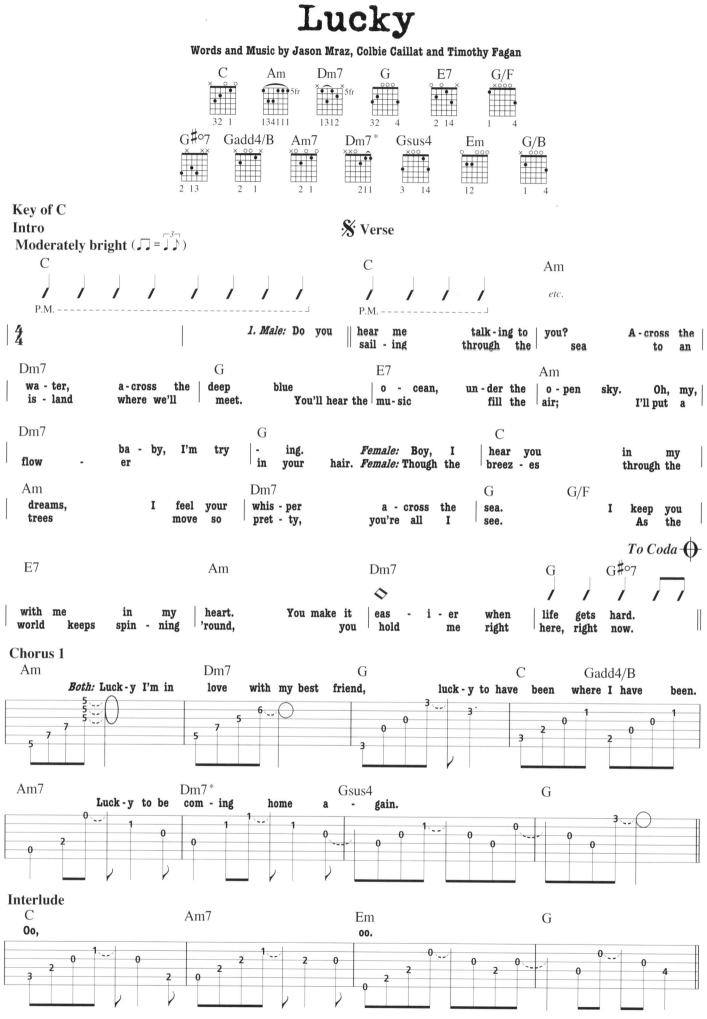

Bridge

Dm7   / / / /   *etc.*   Am7   G   Dm7

Female: They don't know how | long it takes, | wait-ing for a | love like this. |

Male: They don't | know how long it | takes, wait-ing for a | love like this. |

Am7   G   Dm7

Ev - 'ry time we | say good - bye, *Both:* I wish we had | one more kiss. I'll

Ev - 'ry | time we say good - | bye, }

Am7   G   Am7   G/B

wait for you, I | prom - ise you I | will. | I'm ‖

Chorus 2

w/ Chorus pattern

Am   Dm7   G   C   Gadd4/B

| luck - y I'm in | love with my best friend, | luck - y to have | been where I have been. |

Am7   Dm7 *   Gsus4   G   G$\sharp$°7

| Luck - y to be | com - ing home a | - gain. | |

Am   Dm7   G   C   Gadd4/B

| Luck - y we're in | love in ev - 'ry way, | luck - y to have | stayed where we have stayed. |

D.S. al Coda

Am7   Dm7 *   Gsus4   G

| Luck - y to be | com - ing home some | - day. | 2. *Male:* And so I'm ‖

⊕ **Coda**

Chorus 2 (1 time)

Outro

C   Am7

16 / / / / / / / *etc.*

‖: Oo. | |

| 1. | 2. |

Em   G   G   C

oo. | :‖ Oo. | ‖

Makes Me Wonder

Words by Adam Levine
Music by Adam Levine, Jesse Carmichael and Mickey Madden

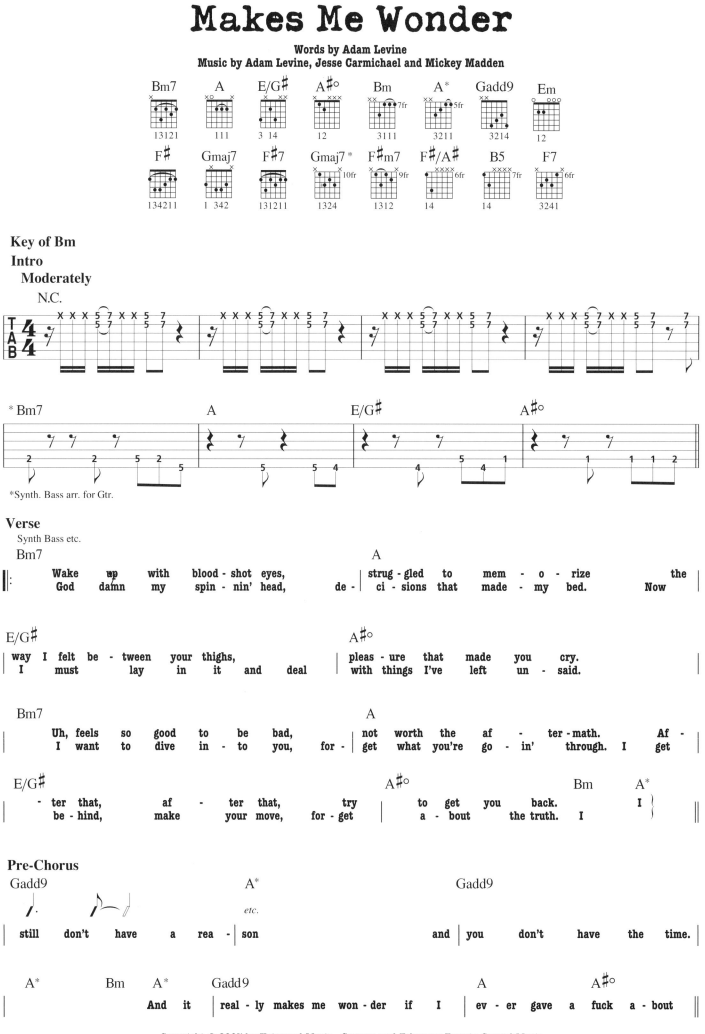

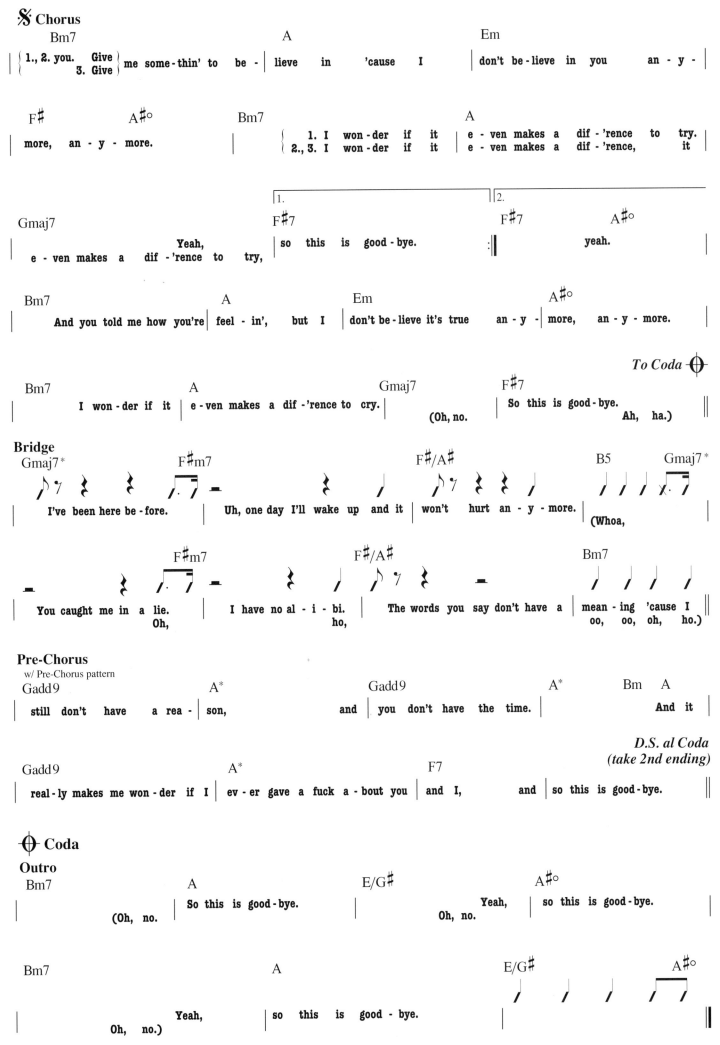

Mercy

Words and Music by Aimee Duffy and Stephen Booker

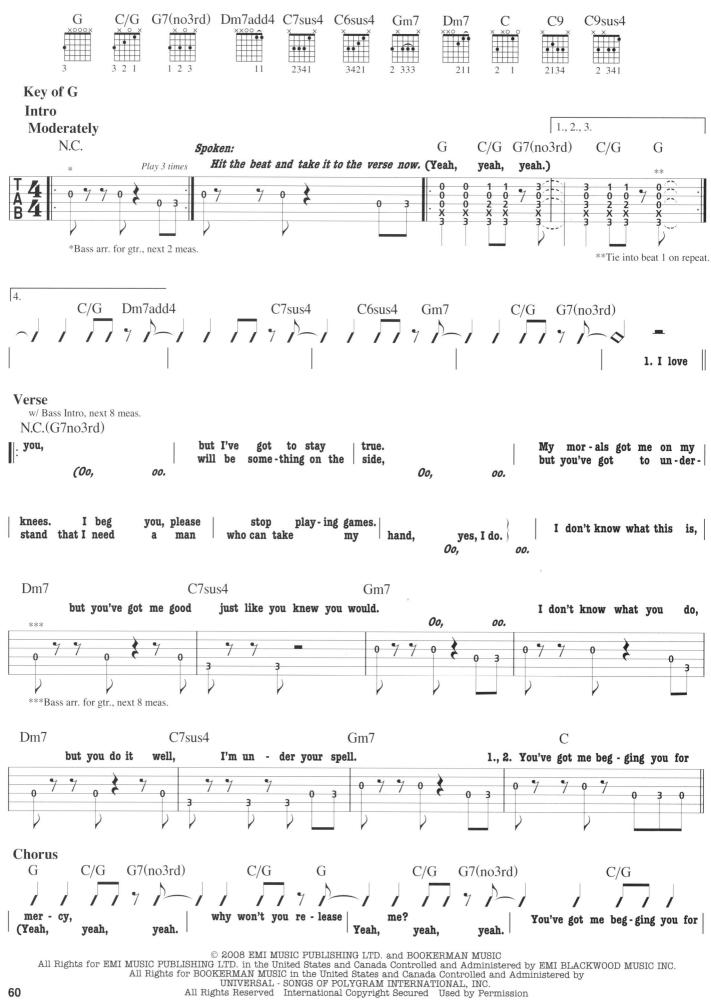

C9		C	C9sus4		C	G		C/G	G7(no3rd)		C/G	

etc.

mer - cy,   why won't you re - lease | me?   I said   re - lease
Yeah,   yeah,   yeah.   Yeah,   yeah,   yeah.

Dm7add4		C9sus4		C C9sus4 C	G		C/G	G7(no3rd)		C/G	

                                                        me.   2. Now you think that I
Yeah,   yeah,   yeah.   Yeah,   yeah,   yeah.)

Bridge

N.C.

I'm   beg - ging   you   for   mer | - cy,   just   why   won't
Spoken: (You   look   and   think   we're   the   same   kind   'cause you don't know   what   I   got   and

you   re - lease | me?   I'm   beg - ging you   for   mer
I   wan-na get more than I'm ask-ing | for, but I just don't want to waste my | time. You know that I'll be the oth-er girl

- cy,   you   got   me   beg   -   ging,
just   like   there's noth - ing   in   this | world.   I   know   that   I'm   gon'   get   me

                                                                                                C

you   got   me   beg   -   ging, | you   got   me   beg   -   ging...
some,   I   just don't know where to get it from.

Chorus

w/ Chorus pattern

G	C/G	G7(no3rd)		C/G	G		C/G	G7(no3rd)		C/G	

: 3. Mer - cy,   why won't you re - lease | me?   I'm beg - ging you for
       mer - cy.   I'm beg - ging you for | mer - cy.   I'm beg - ging you for
    (Yeah,   yeah,   yeah.   Yeah,   yeah,   yeah.

C9		C	C9sus4		C	G		C/G	G7(no3rd)		C/G	

mer   -   cy,   why won't you re - lease | me?   You got me beg-ging you for
mer - cy.   I'm beg - ging you for | mer - cy.   Why won't you re - lease
Yeah,   yeah,   yeah.   Yeah,   yeah,   yeah.

Dm7add4		C9sus4		C C9sus4 C	G		C/G	G7(no3rd)		C/G	

mer   -   cy, | yeah.   4. I'm beg - ging you for :
                                             me,   yeah,   yeah?   Spoken: Break it down.
Yeah,   yeah,   yeah.   Yeah,   yeah,   yeah.)

Outro

w/ Bass Intro, till fade

N.C.(G7no3rd)

Repeat and fade

w/ Lead Voc. ad lib. on repeat

: You got me beg - ging, | beg-ging you for mer - cy. | You got me beg - ging, | down on my knees, I said... :

Mr. Brightside

Words and Music by Brandon Flowers, Dave Keuning, Mark Stoermer and Ronnie Vannucci

Dadd9 Dmaj9/C# Gmaj13 Bm7add4 Dsus2/A G6/9 D5 G5 B5 A5 Asus4 A

Tune down 1/2 step:
(low to high) Eb-Ab-Db-Gb-Bb-Eb

Key of D
Intro
Moderately

Dadd9   Dmaj9/C#   Gmaj13

let ring

Verse
w/ Intro riff, 4 times

Dadd9   Dmaj9/C#   Gmaj13

1. Com - in' out - ta my cage and I've been do - in' just fine. Got - ta, got - ta be down be - cause I want it all.

2. I'm com - in'

Dadd9   Dmaj9/C#   Gmaj13

It start - ed out with a kiss. How did it end up like this? It was on - ly a kiss,

Dadd9   Dmaj9/C#

it was on - ly a kiss. Now I'm fall - ing a - sleep, and she's call - ing a cab

Gmaj13   Dadd9

while he's hav - in' a smoke and she's tak - in' a drag. Now they're go - in' to bed

Dmaj9/C#   Gmaj13

and my stom - ach is sick. And it's all in my head, but she's touch - ing his

Pre-Chorus

Bm7add4   Dsus2/A

chest. Now he takes off her dress. Now let me

G6/9

go.

Bm7add4   **Dsus2/A**

etc.

{ And / 'Cause } I just can't | look; it's | kill - ing me | and |

G⁶₉

tak - ing con | - trol. ‖

Chorus

D5   **G5**   **B5**   **A5**

| Jeal - ous-y, | turn-ing saints in - | to the sea. | Swim-ming through sick |

D5   **G5**   **B5**   **A5**

etc.

| lull - a - bies, | chok - ing on your | al - i-bis, | but it's just the |

D5   **G5**   **B5**   **A5**

| price I pay. | Des - ti - ny is | call - ing me. | O - pen up my |

D5   **G5**   **B5**   **A5**

| ea - ger eyes | | 'cause I'm Mis - ter | Bright - side. ‖

Interlude

etc.

| **D5** | **G5** | **B5** | **A5** | |

1.   2.

| **D5** | **G5** | **B5** | **A5** | **A5** | I ‖

1., 2., 3.   4.

Outro

D5   **G5**   **B5**   **A5**   **A5 Asus4 A**

‖: nev - er. | | | I :‖ ‖

Need You Now

Words and Music by Hillary Scott, Charles Kelley, Dave Haywood and Josh Kear

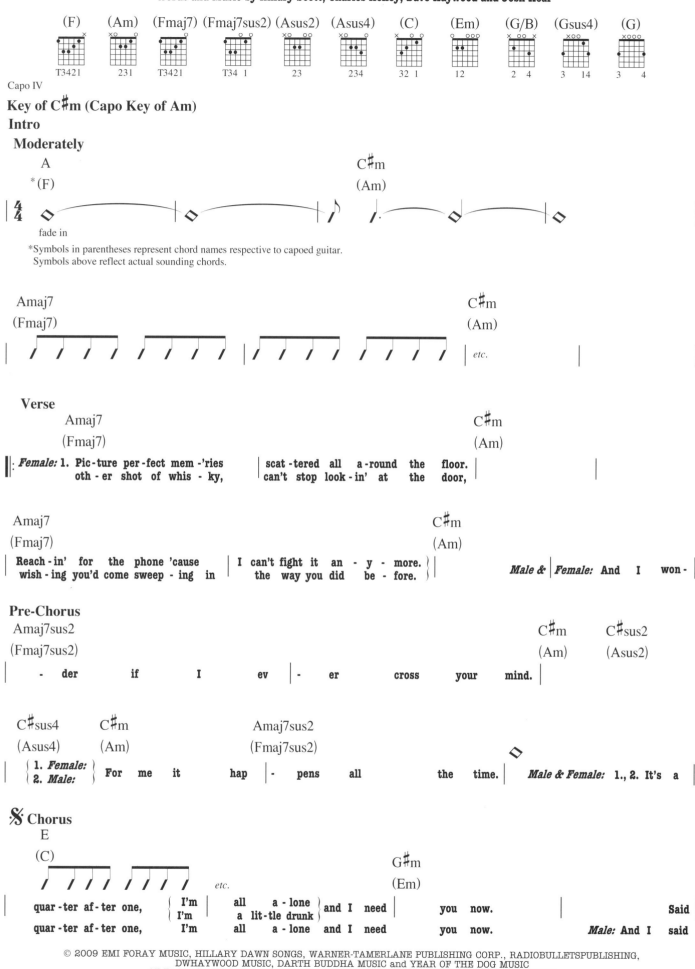

64

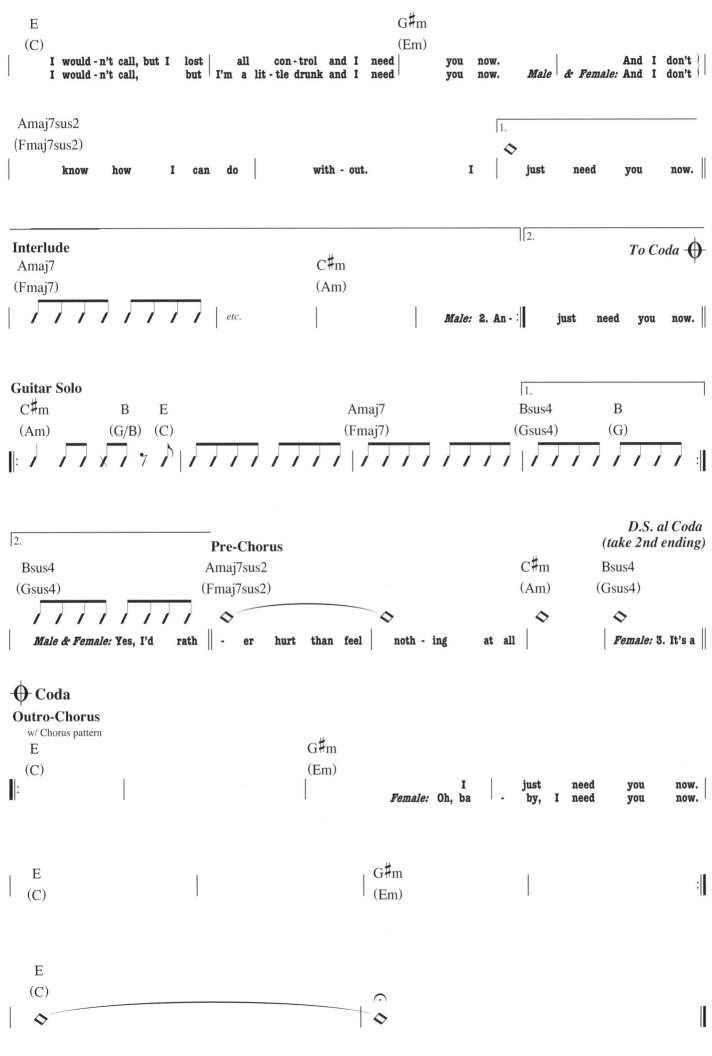

New Divide

Words and Music by Mike Shinoda, Joe Hahn, Brad Delson, Rob Bourdon, Chester Bennington and Dave Farrell

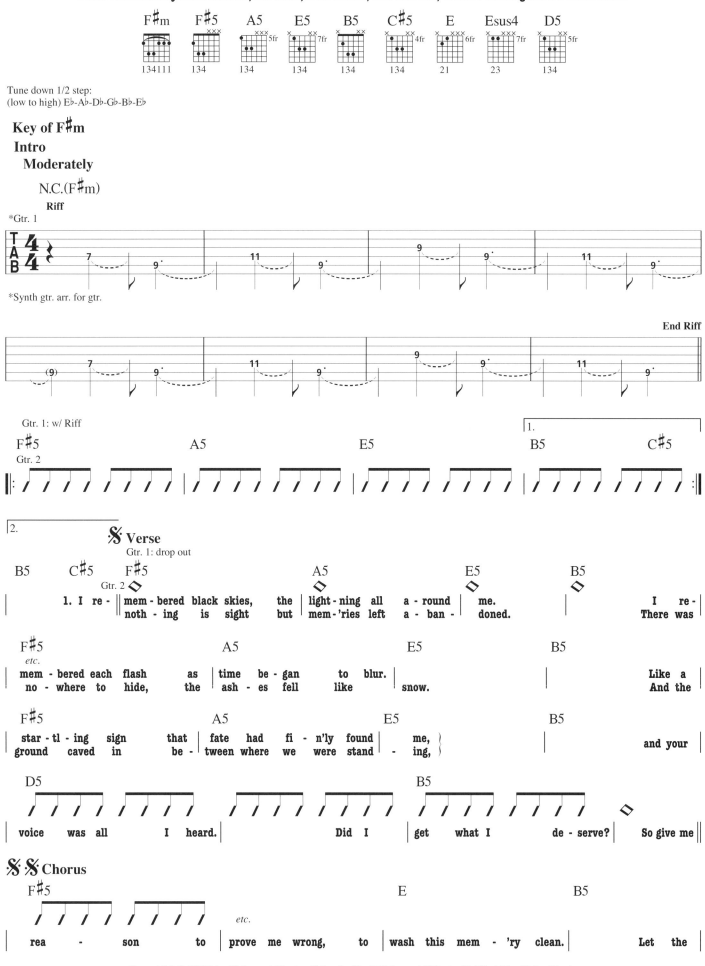

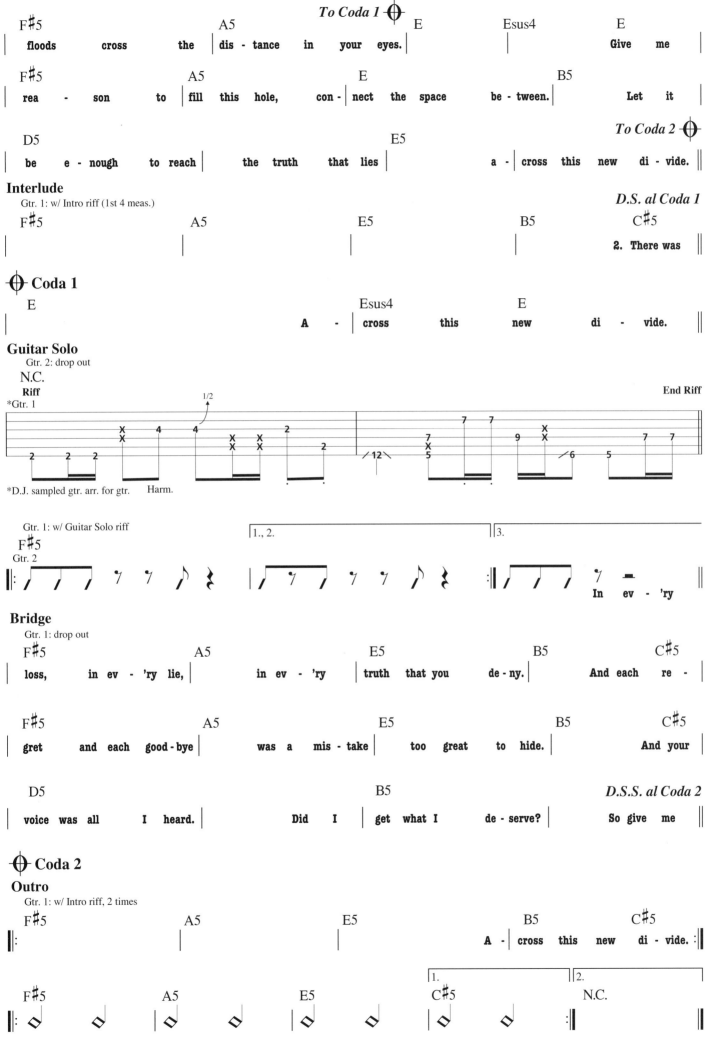

Sex on Fire

Words and Music by Caleb Followill, Nathan Followill, Jared Followill and Matthew Followill

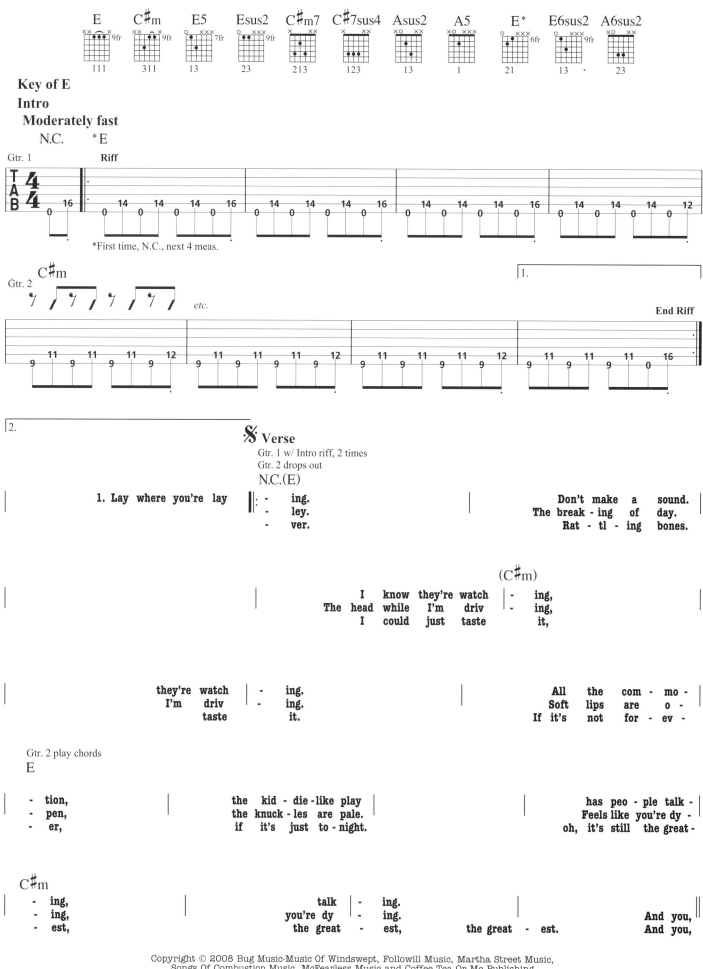

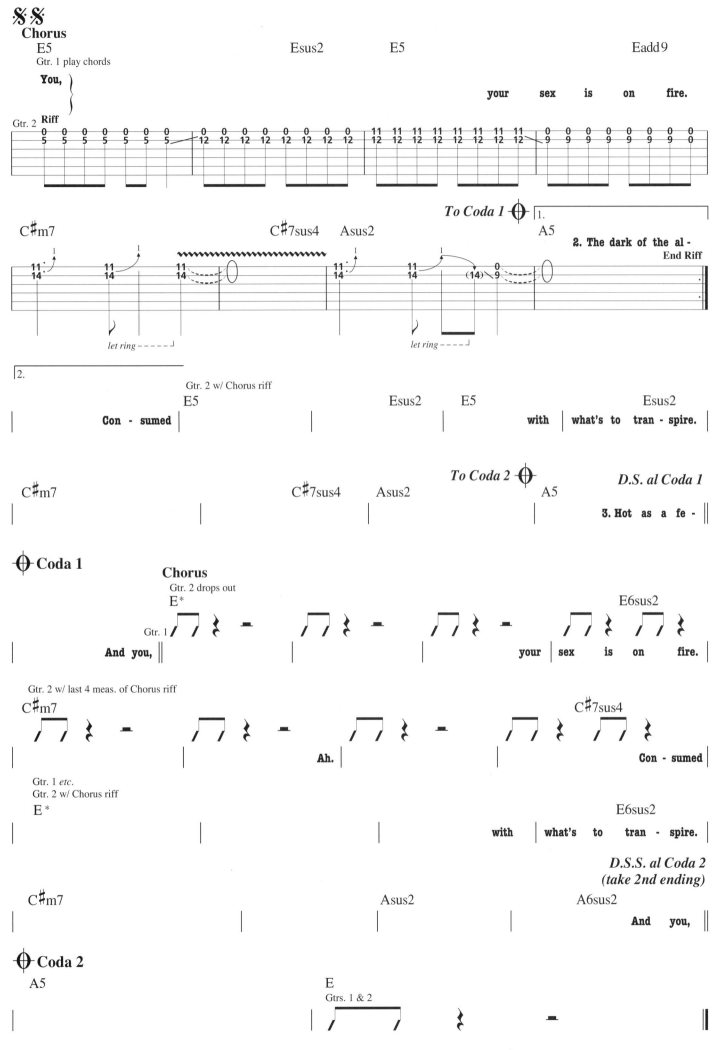

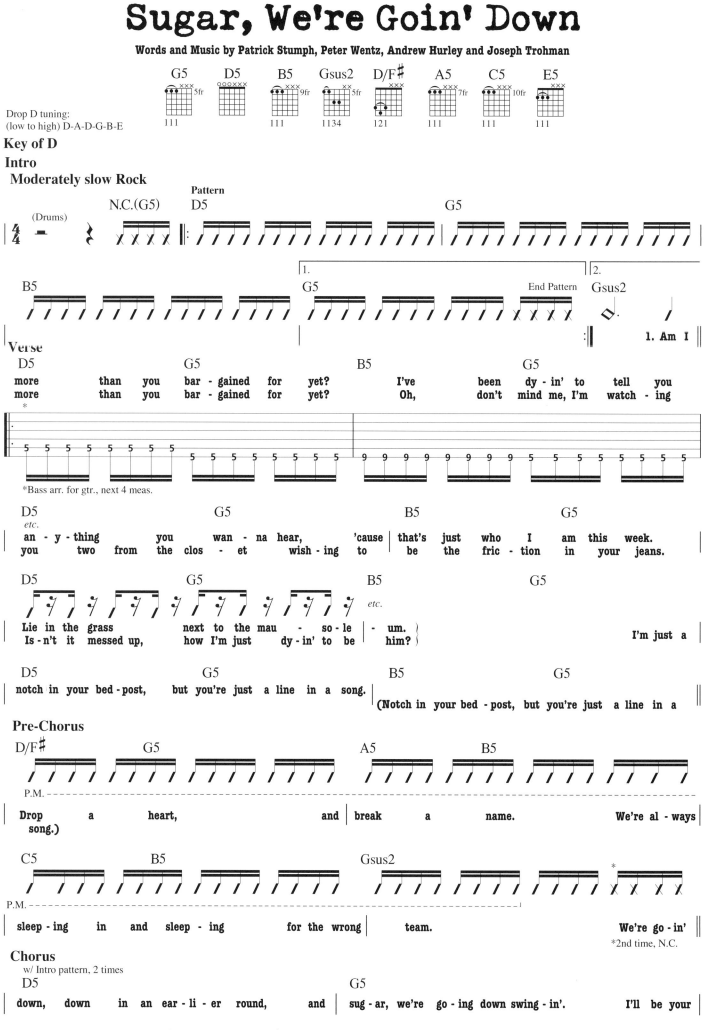

Sugar, We're Goin' Down

Words and Music by Patrick Stumph, Peter Wentz, Andrew Hurley and Joseph Trohman

Take Me Out

Words and Music by Alex Kapranos and Nick McCarthy

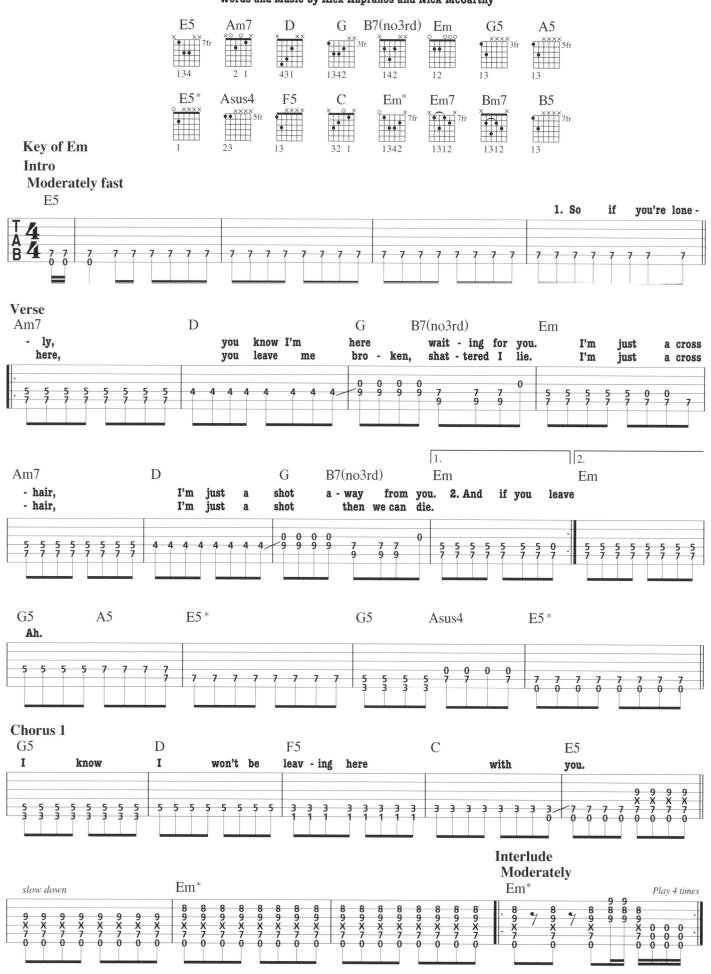

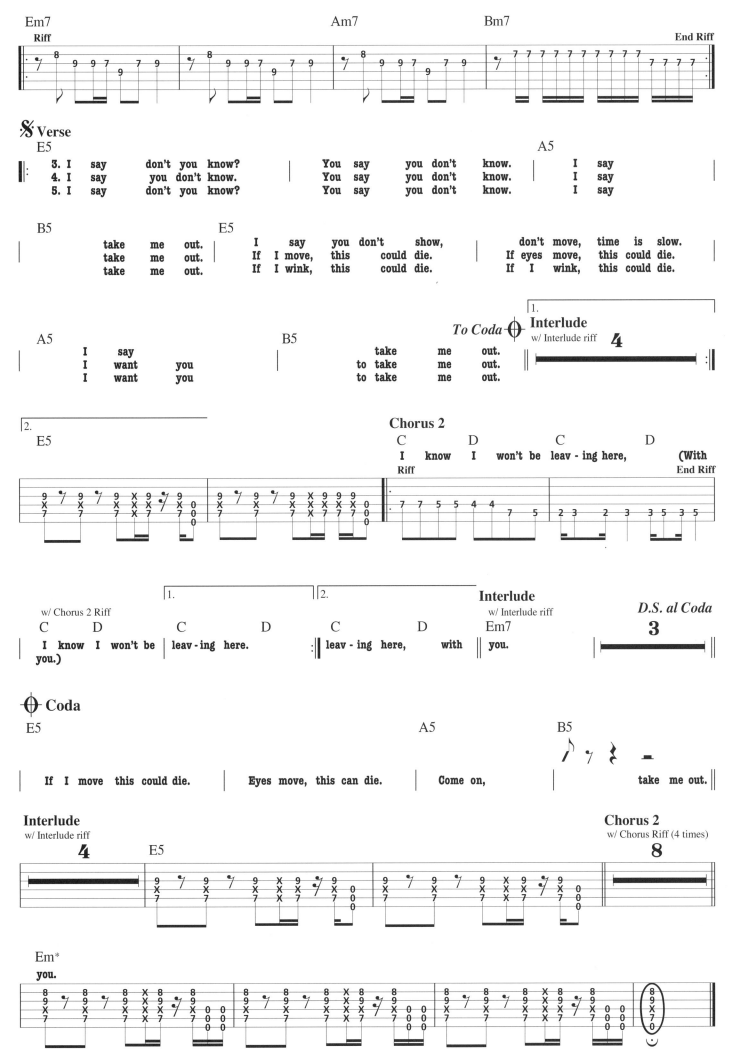

Toes

Words and Music by Shawn Mullins, Zac Brown, Wyatt Durrette and John Hopkins

Tune down 1/2 step:
(low to high) Eb-Ab-Db-Gb-Bb-Eb

Key of C

Intro

Moderately

w/ fingers

let ring

let ring

Refrain

fingerpick or strum

C	F/C	C C/B Am	G C/G G
toes in the wa - ter, ass	in the sand. Not a wor -	ry in the world, a cold	beer in my hand. Life is good

F	Gsus4		C
to - day,	life is good to - day.		1. Well, the plane

Verse

C	F/C	C	G5
touched down just a - bout	three o' - clock and the cit	- y's still on my mind.	Bi -
flew by like a drunk	Fri - day night as the sum	- mer drew to an end.	They

C	F/C	C G5	C
ki - nis and palm trees danced	in my head, I was still	in the bag - gage line.	Con -
can't be - lieve that I just	could-n't leave and I bid	a - dieu to my friends.	'Cause my

	F/C	C	G5
- crete and cars are their own	pris - on bars like this	life I'm liv - in' in.	But the
bar - tend - er, she's	from the is - lands. Her	bod-y's been kissed by the sun.	And

C	F/C	C G5	C
plane brought me far - ther, I'm sur -	round - ed by wa - ter and I'm	not go - in' back a - gain.	I got my
co - co - nut re - plac - es the smell	of the bar and I don't	know if it's her or the rum.	

Refrain

C	F	C C/B Am	G C/G G
toes in the wa - ter, ass	in the sand. Not a wor -	ry in the world, a cold	beer in my hand. Life is good

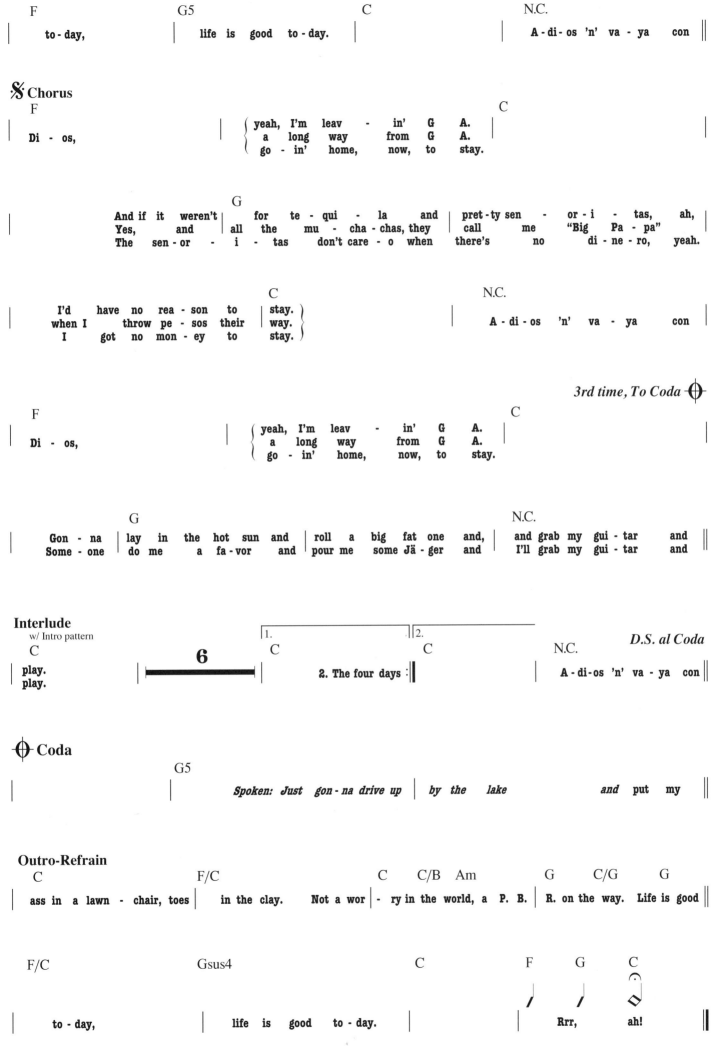

21 Guns

Words and Music by David Bowie, John Phillips, Billie Joe Armstrong, Mike Pritchard and Frank Wright

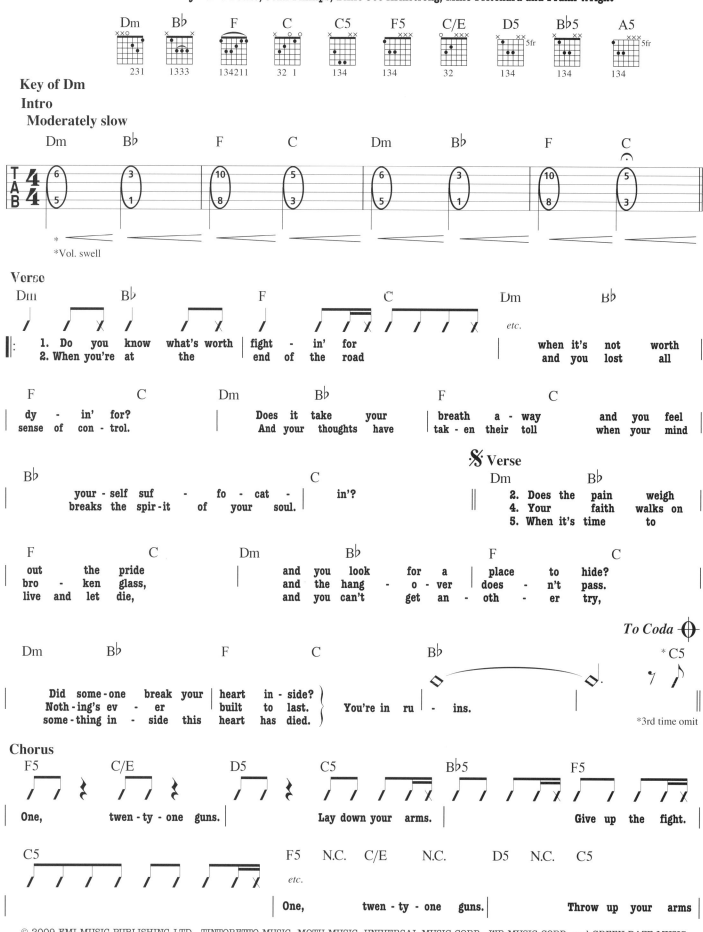

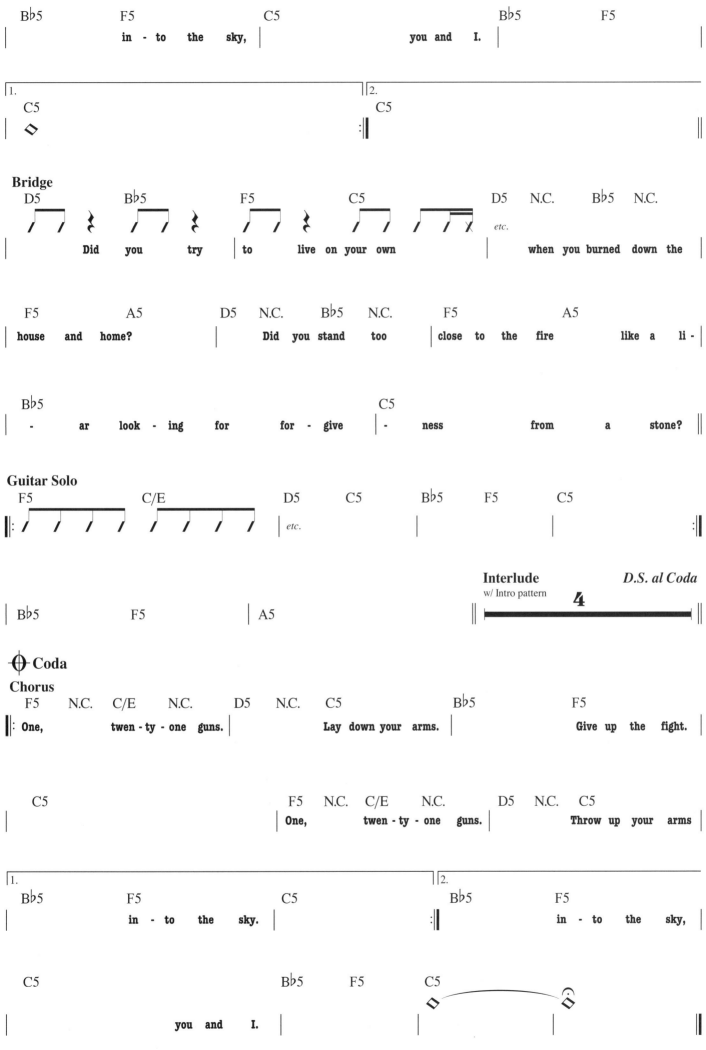

Use Somebody

Words and Music by Caleb Followill, Nathan Followill, Jared Followill and Matthew Followill

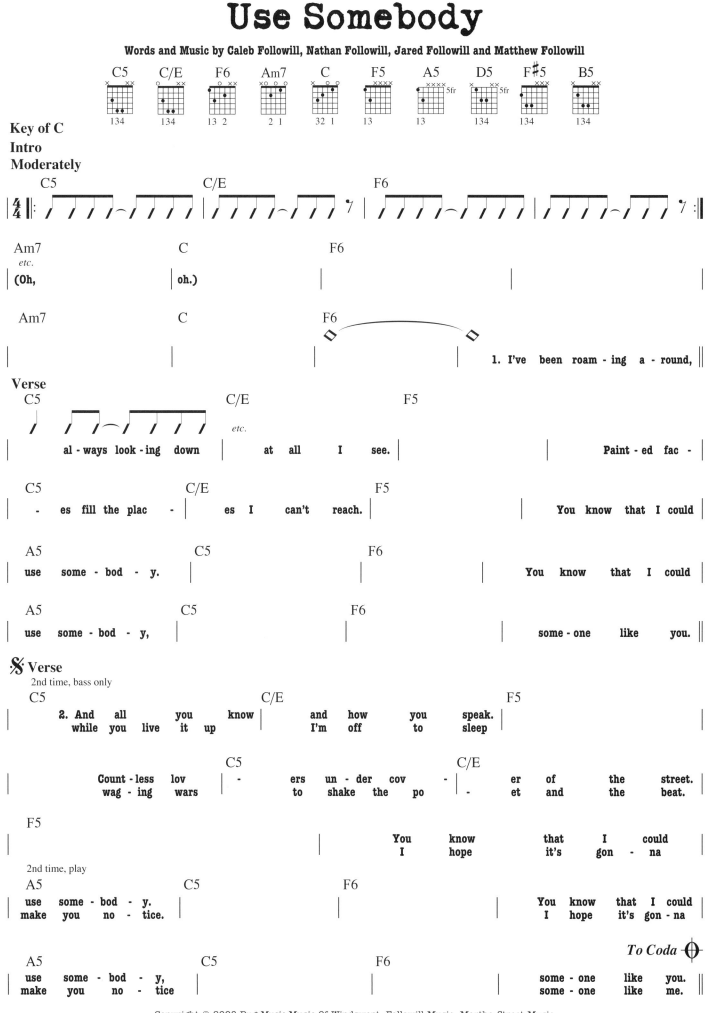

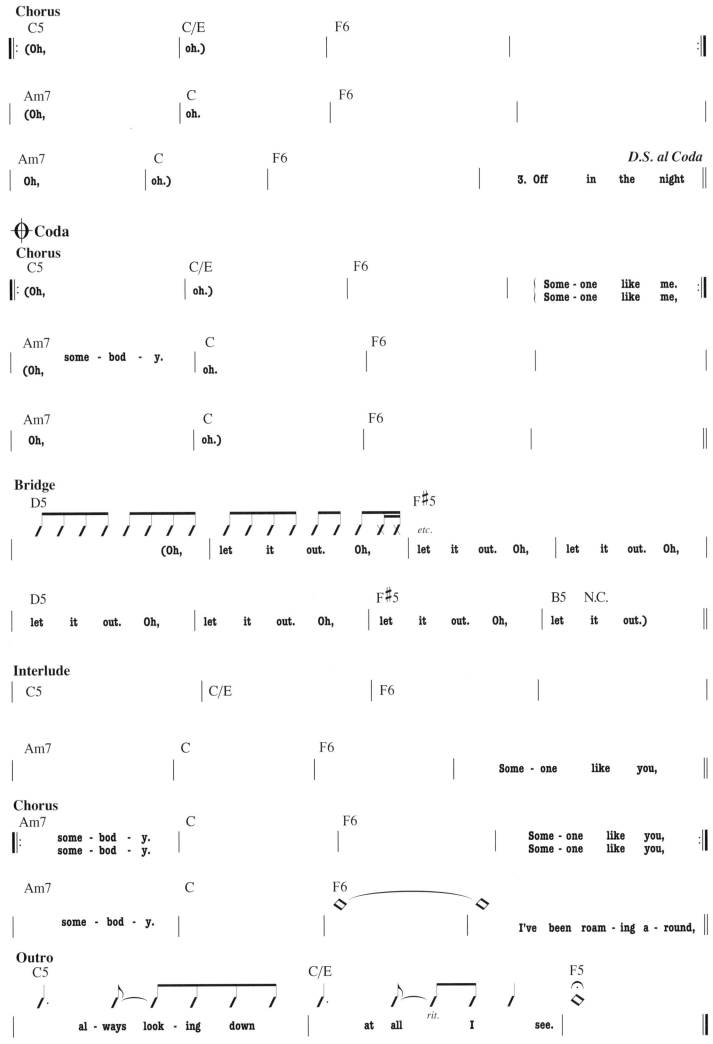

Viva la Vida

Words and Music by Guy Berryman, Jon Buckland, Will Champion and Chris Martin

(C5) (D7sus4) (G) (Em) (G/B) (Cmaj7) (Gmaj7)

Capo I

Key of A♭ (Capo Key of G)

Intro

Moderately

| D♭5 | E♭7sus4 | A♭ | Fm | 1. | 2. |
| *(C5) | (D7sus4) | (G) | (Em) | | |

w/ fingers
Strings arr. for gtr.

*Symbols in parentheses represent chord names respective to capoed guitar.
Symbols above reflect actual sounding chords. Capoed fret in "0" in tab.

Verse

D♭5	E♭7sus4		A♭	Fm
(C5)	(D7sus4)		(G)	(Em)
etc.				
rule	the world.	Seas would	rise when I gave the word.	Now in the morn - ing I

D♭5	E♭7sus4		A♭	Fm
(C5)	(D7sus4)		(G)	(Em)
sleep	a - lone,	sweep the	streets I used to own.	

Interlude

| D♭5 | E♭7sus4 | A♭ | Fm | 1. | 2. |
| (C5) | (D7sus4) | (G) | (Em) | | |

2. I used to
3. It was the wick - ed and wild

Verse

D♭5	E♭7sus4		A♭	Fm
(C5)	(D7sus4)		(G)	(Em)
roll	the dice,	feel the	fear in my en - e - my's eyes.	Lis - ten as the
	wind	blew down the	doors to let me in.	Shat - tered win - dows and the

D♭5	E♭7sus4		A♭	Fm
(C5)	(D7sus4)		(G)	(Em)
crowd	would sing,	"Now the	old king is dead, long live	the king." One min - ute I
sound	of drums.	Peo - ple	could - n't be - lieve what I'd	be - come. Rev - o - lu - tion-

D♭5	E♭7sus4		A♭	Fm
(C5)	(D7sus4)		(G)	(Em)
held	the key,	next the	walls were closed on	me. And I dis - cov - ered that my
ar -	ies wait	for my	head on a sil - ver plate.	Just a pup - pet on a

D♭5	E♭7sus4		A♭	Fm
(C5)	(D7sus4)		(G)	(Em)
cas -	tles stand	up - on	pil - lars of salt and pil - lars	of sand.
lone -	ly string.	Ah,	who would ev - er want to be King?	I

Copyright © 2008 by Universal Music Publishing MGB Ltd.
All Rights in the United States and Canada Administered by Universal Music - MGB Songs
International Copyright Secured   All Rights Reserved

𝄋 𝄋

Chorus
strum chords

D♭5	E♭7sus4		A♭	Fm
(C5)	(D7sus4)		(G)	(Em)

| hear Je - ru - sa - lem bells | a ring - ing. | Ro - man Cal - va - ry choirs | are sing - ing. |

D♭5	E♭7sus4		A♭	Fm
(C5)	(D7sus4)		(G)	(Em)

| Be my mir - ror, my sword | and shield, my | mis - sion - ar - ies in a for | - eign field. |

D♭5	E♭7sus4		A♭/C	Fm
(C5)	(D7sus4)		(G/B)	(Em)

| For some rea - son I can't | ex - plain, | 1. once you'd gone there was | nev - er, nev - er an hon - |
| | | | 2, 3. I know Saint Pe - ter won't call | my name, nev - er |

To Coda 1 ⊕

To Coda 2 ⊕   *D.S. al Coda 1*
                    (take repeat)

D♭maj7	E♭7sus4		A♭maj7	Fm
(Cmaj7)	(D7sus4)		(Gmaj7)	(Em)

| - est word. | And that was | when I ruled the world. |
| an hon - est word. | But that was | when I ruled the world. |

⊕ **Coda 1**

Bridge

D♭5	Fm		E♭7sus4	
(C5)	(Em)		(D7sus4)	

Play 3 times   Oh,

D♭5	E♭7sus4		A♭	Fm
(C5)	(D7sus4)		(G)	(Em)

2nd time, D.S.S. al Coda 2

| oh, | oh, | oh. I |
| oh, | | |

⊕ **Coda 2**

Outro   *Repeat and fade*

D♭5	E♭7sus4	A♭	Fm
(C5)	(D7sus4)	(G)	(Em)

| Oo. | | | |

81

What About Now

Words and Music by David Hodges, Ben Moody and Josh Hartzler

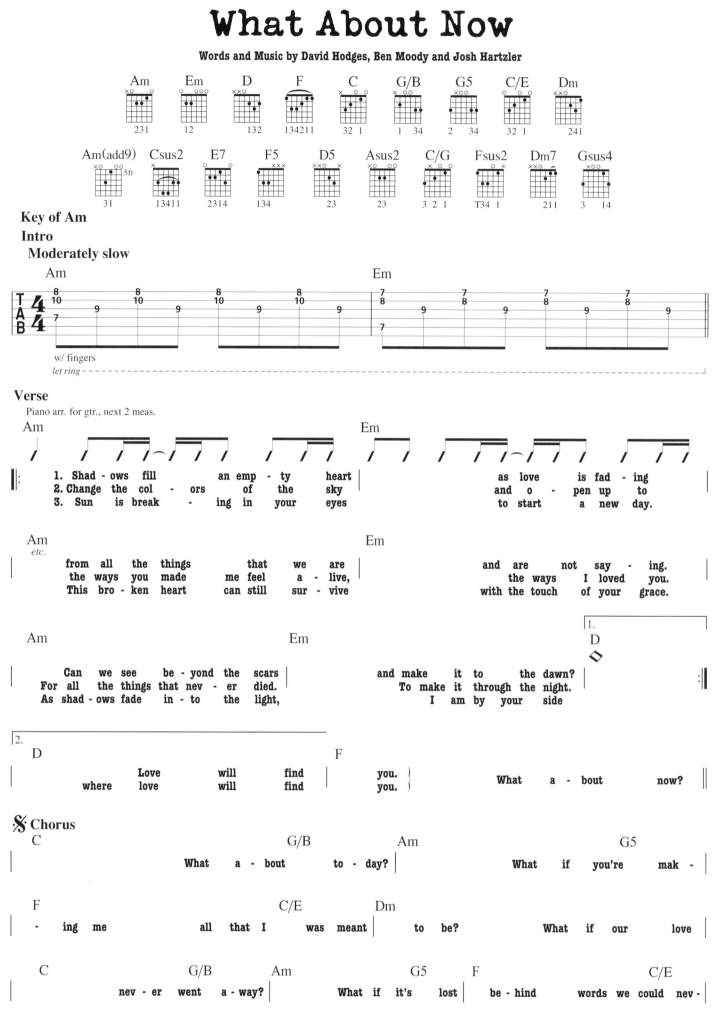

To Coda 1 ⊕

To Coda 2 ⊕

D.C. al Coda 1
(take 2nd ending)

Dm	C/E	F
- er find? Ba - by, be - fore	it's too late,	what a - bout now? ‖

⊕ **Coda 1**

Bridge

F	Dm	Am(add9)
what a - bout now, ‖	now that we're here?	Now that we've come

Csus2	E7	Dm
this far, just hold	on.	There is noth - ing to fear,

Am(add9)	F5	
for I am right	be - side	you. For all

D5	Asus2	
my life	I am yours.	What a - bout now? ‖

Chorus

Am	C/G	
What a - bout to - day?	What if you're mak -

Fsus2	C/E Dm7	
- ing me all that I was meant	to be?	What if our love,

Am	Gsus4	
it nev - er went a - way?	What if it's lost

Fsus2	G5	*D.S. al Coda 2*
be - hind words we could nev	- er find?	What a - bout now? ‖

⊕ **Coda 2**

F	C/E	F
ba - by, be - fore	it's too late,	ba - by, be - fore

C/E	F	
it's too late,	what a - bout now?	‖

83

What Hurts the Most

Words and Music by Steve Robson and Jeffrey Steele

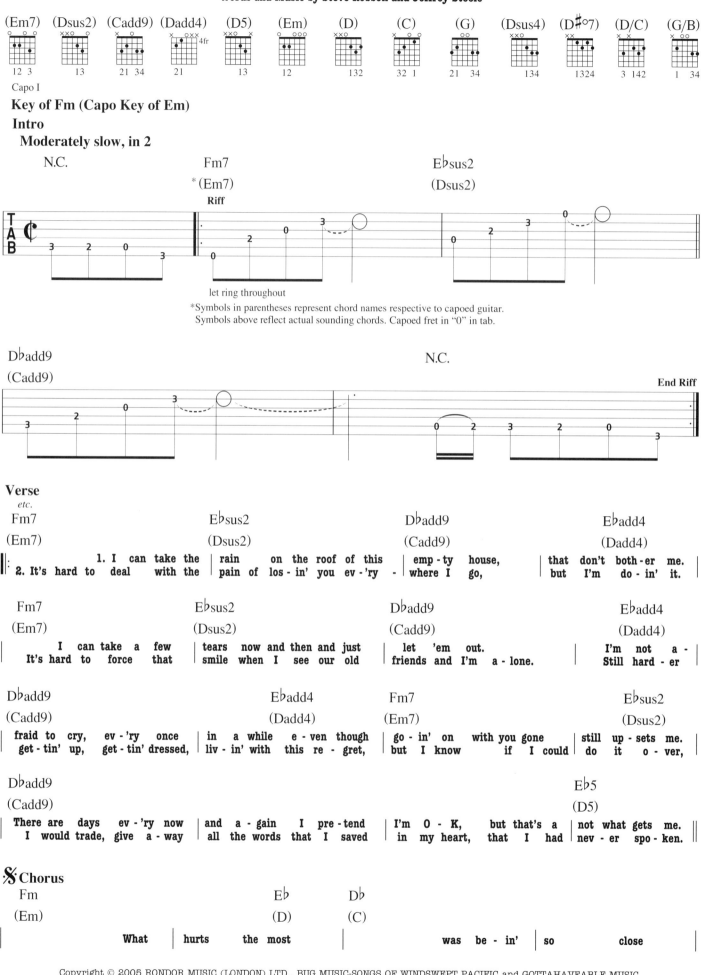

Key of Fm (Capo Key of Em)

Intro

Moderately slow, in 2

*Symbols in parentheses represent chord names respective to capoed guitar.
Symbols above reflect actual sounding chords. Capoed fret in "0" in tab.

Verse
etc.

1. I can take the rain on the roof of this empty house, that don't bother me.
2. It's hard to deal with the pain of losin' you ev'rywhere I go, but I'm doin' it.

I can take a few tears now and then and just let 'em out. I'm not a-
It's hard to force that smile when I see our old friends and I'm alone. Still harder

fraid to cry, ev'ry once in a while even though go-in' on with you gone still upsets me.
gettin' up, gettin' dressed, livin' with this regret, but I know if I could do it over,

There are days ev'ry now and again I pretend I'm O-K, but that's a not what gets me.
I would trade, give away all the words that I saved in my heart, that I had never spoken.

Chorus

Fm   Eb   Db
(Em)   (D) (C)

What hurts the most was bein' so close

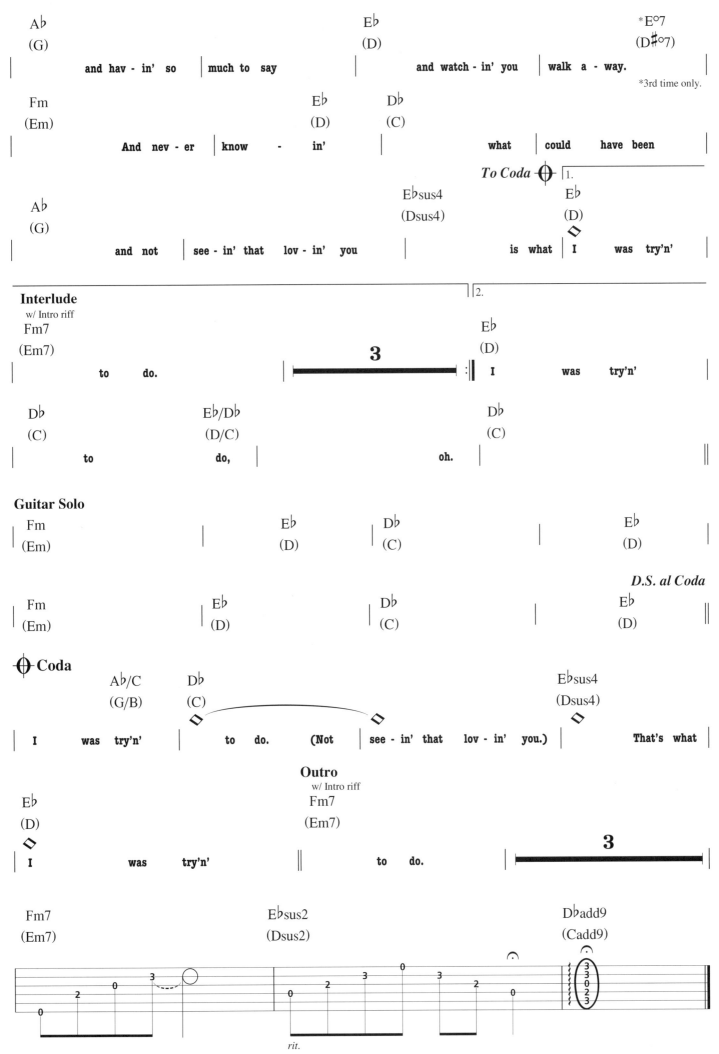

When You're Gone

Words and Music by Avril Lavigne and Butch Walker

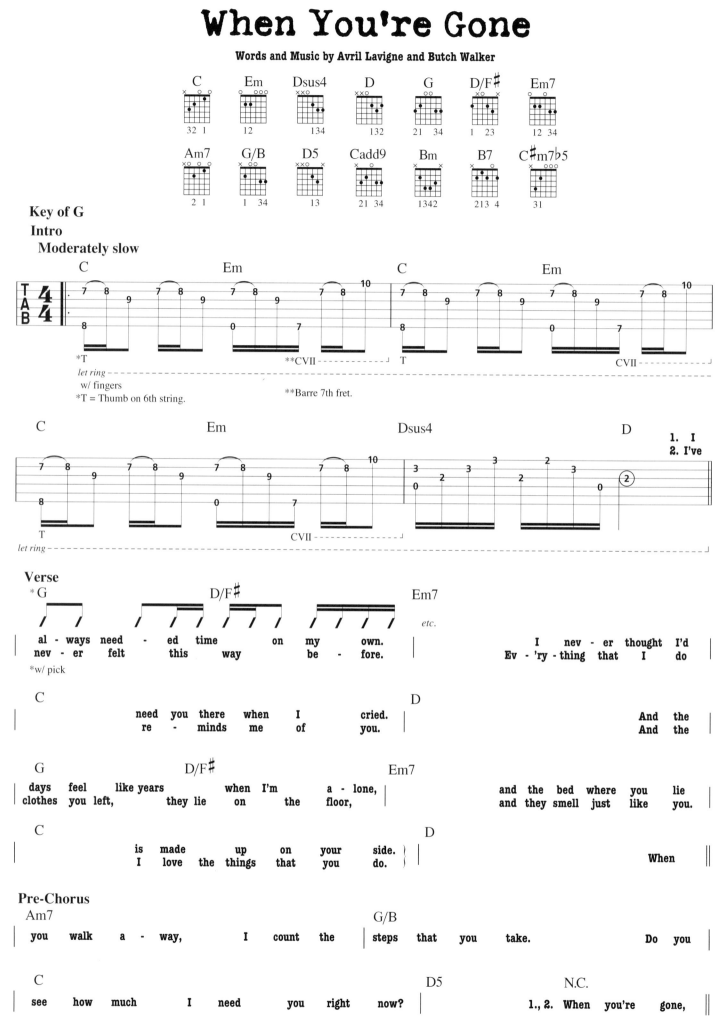

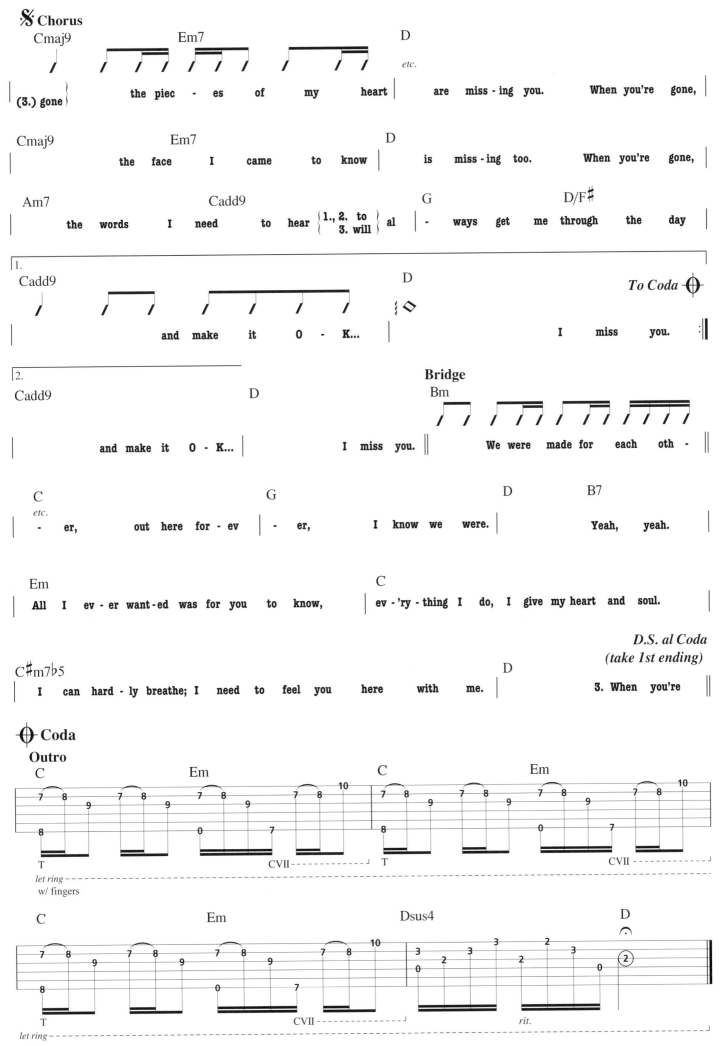

You Belong with Me

Words and Music by Taylor Swift and Liz Rose

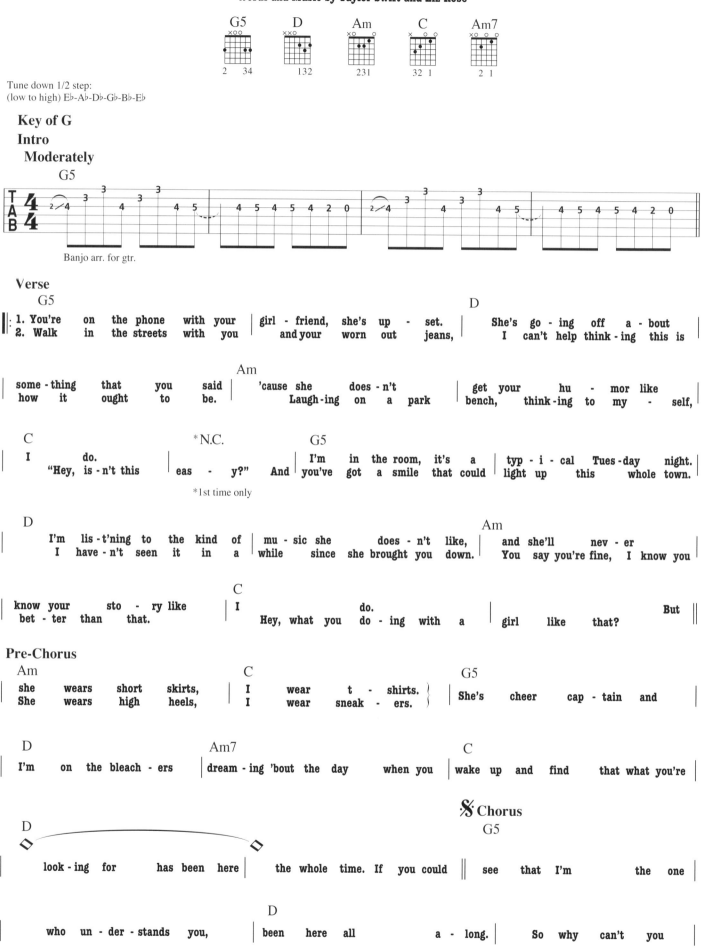

*Am   1.
                                            C

| see, | ee, | you be - long with | me, | ee? | You be - long with me. |

*3rd time, let chord ring

Interlude
w/ Intro riff
G5   2.
                              C   G5

| | | me, | ee. | | Stand - ing by, | wait - |

D

| - ing at your back door. | All this time, how could | you not know? Ba - |

                                                To Coda ⊕

Am   C

| by, | ee, | you be - long with | me, | ee. | You be - long with me. |

Guitar Solo
| G5 | | | D | | |

| Am | | C | | | |
| | | | | Oh, | I re - mem - ber you |

Bridge
Am   C   G5

| driv - ing to my house in the | mid - dle of the night. I'm the | one who makes you laugh when you |

D   Am   C

| know you're 'bout to cry. I | know your fa - v'rite songs and you | tell me 'bout your dreams. Think I |

                                              D.S. al Coda
                                            (take 2nd ending)

G5   D

| know where you be - long, think I | know it's with me. | | Can't you |

⊕ **Coda**
Outro
G5   D

| | You be - long with | me. | Have you |

                                    Am

| ev - er thought just may - | be, | ee, | you be - long with |

C   G5

| me, | ee? | You be - long with me. | |

You're Beautiful

Words and Music by James Blunt, Sacha Skarbek and Amanda Ghost

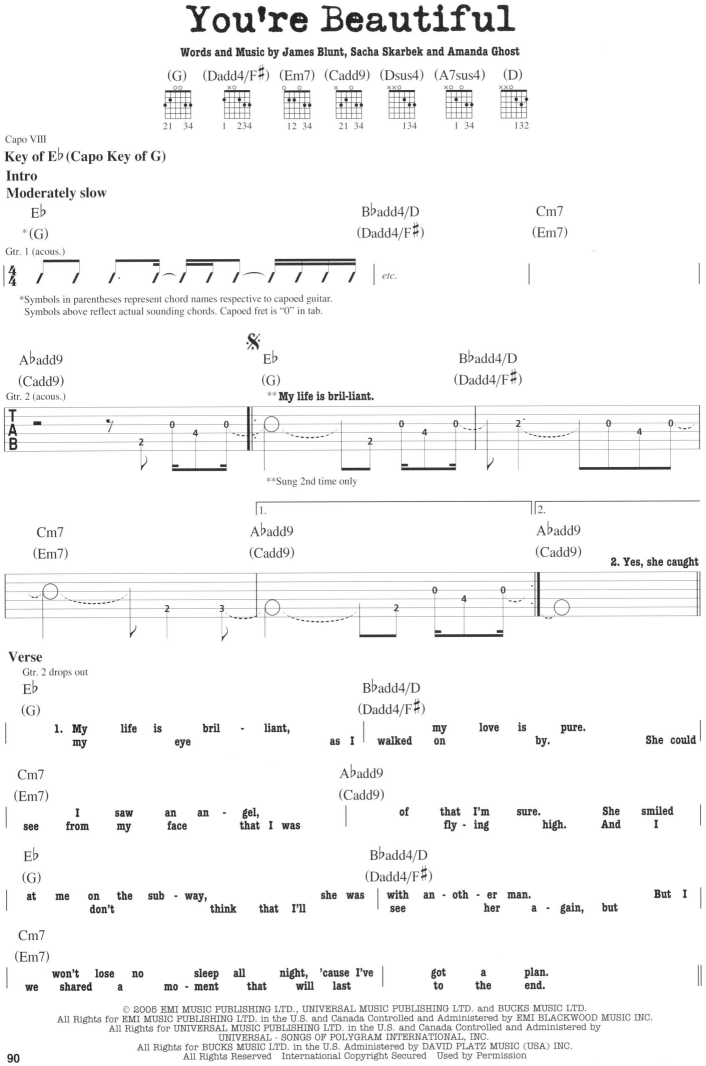

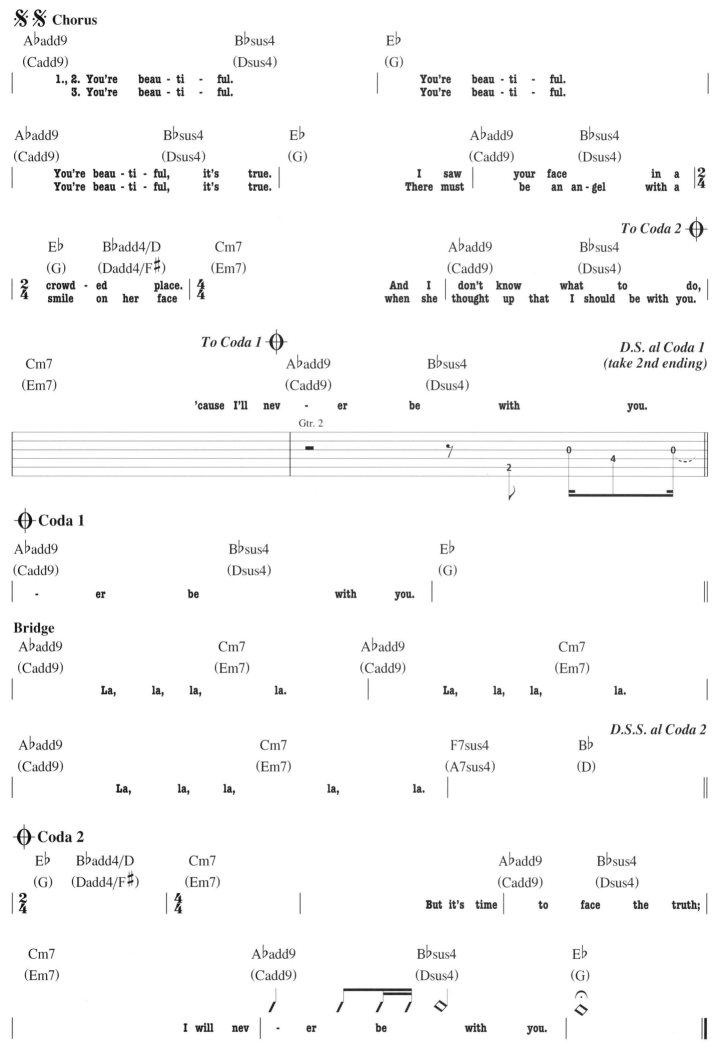

RHYTHM TAB LEGEND

Rhythm Tab is a form of notation that adds rhythmic values to the traditional tab staff.

TABLATURE graphically represents the guitar fingerboard. Each horizontal line represents a string, and each number represents a fret. Rhythmic values are shown using ovals, stems, and dots.

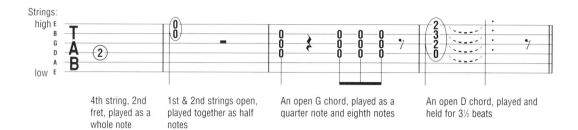

4th string, 2nd fret, played as a whole note

1st & 2nd strings open, played together as half notes

An open G chord, played as a quarter note and eighth notes

An open D chord, played and held for 3½ beats

Definitions for Special Guitar Notation

HALF-STEP BEND: Strike the note and bend up 1/2 step.

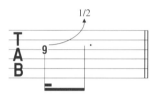

WHOLE-STEP BEND: Strike the note and bend up one step.

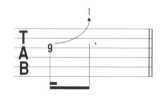

GRACE NOTE BEND: Strike the note and immediately bend up as indicated.

SLIGHT (MICROTONE) BEND: Strike the note and bend up 1/4 step.

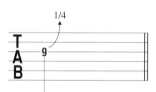

BEND AND RELEASE: Strike the note and bend up as indicated, then release back to the original note. Only the first note is struck.

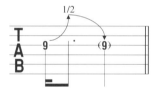

PRE-BEND: Bend the note as indicated, then strike it.

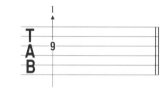

PRE-BEND AND RELEASE: Bend the note as indicated. Strike it and release the bend back to the original note.

UNISON BEND: Strike the two notes simultaneously and bend the lower note up to the pitch of the higher.

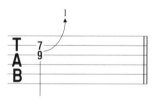

HOLD BEND: While sustaining bent note, strike note on different string.

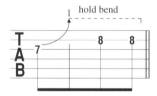

VIBRATO: The string is vibrated by rapidly bending and releasing the note with the fretting hand.

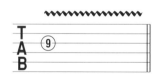

WIDE VIBRATO: The pitch is varied to a greater degree by vibrating with the fretting hand.

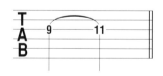

HAMMER-ON: Strike the first (lower) note with one finger, then sound the higher note (on the same string) with another finger by fretting it without picking.

PULL-OFF: Place both fingers on the notes to be sounded. Strike the first note and without picking, pull the finger off to sound the second (lower) note.

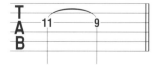

HAMMER FROM NOWHERE: Sound note(s) by hammering with fret hand finger only.

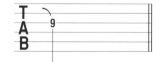

GRACE NOTE SLUR: Strike the note and immediately hammer-on (or pull-off) as indicated.

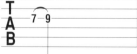

GRACE NOTE SLUR (CLUSTER): Strike the notes and immediately hammer-on (or pull-off) as indicated.

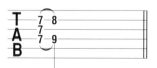

LEGATO SLIDE: Strike the first note and then slide the same fret-hand finger up or down to the second note. The second note is not struck.

SHIFT SLIDE: Same as legato slide, except the second note is struck.

TRILL: Very rapidly alternate between the notes indicated by continuously hammering on and pulling off.

TAPPING: Hammer ("tap") the fret indicated with the pick-hand index or middle finger and pull off to the note fretted by the fret hand.

NATURAL HARMONIC: Strike the note while the fret-hand lightly touches the string directly over the fret indicated.

Harm.

PINCH HARMONIC: The note is fretted normally and a harmonic is produced by adding the edge of the thumb or the tip of the index finger of the pick hand to the normal pick attack.

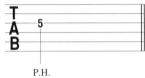

P.H.

HARP HARMONIC: The note is fretted normally and a harmonic is produced by gently resting the pick hand's index finger directly above the indicated fret (in parentheses) while the pick hand's thumb or pick assists by plucking the appropriate string.

H.H.

PICK SCRAPE: The edge of the pick is rubbed down (or up) the string, producing a scratchy sound.

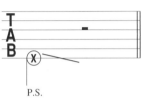

P.S.

MUFFLED STRINGS: A percussive sound is produced by laying the fret hand across the string(s) without depressing, and striking them with the pick hand.

PALM MUTING: The note is partially muted by the pick hand lightly touching the string(s) just before the bridge.

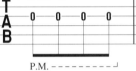

P.M. - - - - - - - -

RAKE: Drag the pick across the strings indicated with a single motion.

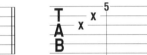

rake - - ⌐

TREMOLO PICKING: The note is picked as rapidly and continuously as possible.

ARPEGGIATE: Play the notes of the chord indicated by quickly rolling them from bottom to top.

VIBRATO BAR DIVE AND RETURN: The pitch of the note or chord is dropped a specified number of steps (in rhythm), then returned to the original pitch.

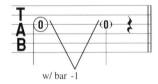

w/ bar -1

VIBRATO BAR SCOOP: Depress the bar just before striking the note, then quickly release the bar.

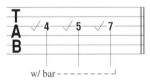

w/ bar - - - - - - - ⌐

VIBRATO BAR DIP: Strike the note and then immediately drop a specified number of steps, then release back to the original pitch.

w/ bar - - - - - - ⌐

Additional Musical Definitions

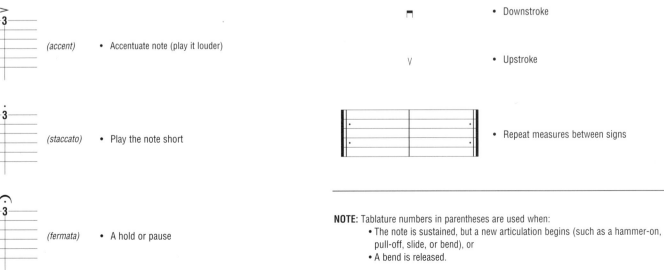

(accent) • Accentuate note (play it louder)

(staccato) • Play the note short

(fermata) • A hold or pause

• Downstroke

• Upstroke

• Repeat measures between signs

NOTE: Tablature numbers in parentheses are used when:
• The note is sustained, but a new articulation begins (such as a hammer-on, pull-off, slide, or bend), or
• A bend is released.

Guitar Chord Songbooks

Each 6" x 9" book includes complete lyrics, chord symbols, and guitar chord diagrams.

Acoustic Rock
00699540 . . . . $17.95

Alabama
00699914 . . . . $14.95

The Beach Boys
00699566 . . . . $14.95

The Beatles (A-I)
00699558 . . . . $17.99

The Beatles (J-Y)
00699562 . . . . $17.99

Blues
00699733 . . . . $12.95

Broadway
00699920 . . . . $14.99

Johnny Cash
00699648 . . . . $16.95

Steven Curtis Chapman
00700702 . . . . $17.99

Children's Songs
00699539 . . . . $14.95

Christmas Carols
00699536 . . . . $12.95

Christmas Songs
00699537 . . . . $12.95

Eric Clapton
00699567 . . . . $15.99

Classic Rock
00699598 . . . . $15.99

Contemporary Christian
00699564 . . . . $14.95

Country
00699534 . . . . $14.95

Country Favorites
00700609 . . . . $14.99

Country Standards
00700608 . . . . $12.95

Cowboy Songs
00699636 . . . . $12.95

Crosby, Stills & Nash
00701609 . . . . $12.99

Neil Diamond
00700606 . . . . $14.99

Disney
00701071 . . . . $14.99

The Doors
00699888 . . . . $15.99

Early Rock
00699916 . . . . $14.99

Folksongs
00699541 . . . . $12.95

Folk Pop Rock
00699651 . . . . $14.95

Four Chord Songs
00701611 . . . . $12.99

Gospel Hymns
00700463 . . . . $14.99

Grand Ole Opry®
00699885 . . . . $16.95

Hillsong United
00700222 . . . . $12.95

Irish Songs
00701044 . . . . $14.99

Jazz Standards
00700972 . . . . $14.99

Billy Joel
00699632 . . . . $15.99

Elton John
00699732 . . . . $15.99

Latin Songs
00700973 . . . . $14.99

Love Songs
00701043 . . . . $14.99

Paul McCartney
00385035 . . . . $16.95

Steve Miller
00701146 . . . . $12.99

Motown
00699734 . . . . $16.95

The 1950s
00699922 . . . . $14.99

The 1980s
00700551 . . . . $16.99

Nirvana
00699762 . . . . $16.99

Roy Orbison
00699752 . . . . $12.95

Tom Petty
00699883 . . . . $15.99

Pop/Rock
00699538 . . . . $14.95

Praise & Worship
00699634 . . . . $12.95

Elvis Presley
00699633 . . . . $14.95

Red Hot Chili Peppers
00699710 . . . . $16.95

Rock Ballads
00701034 . . . . $14.99

Rock 'n' Roll
00699535 . . . . $14.95

Bob Seger
00701147 . . . . $12.99

Taylor Swift
00701799 . . . . $14.99

Sting
00699921 . . . . $14.99

Three Chord Songs
00699720 . . . . $12.95

Wedding Songs
00701005 . . . . $14.99

Hank Williams
00700607 . . . . $14.99

FOR MORE INFORMATION, SEE YOUR LOCAL MUSIC DEALER,
OR WRITE TO:

HAL•LEONARD®
CORPORATION
7777 W. BLUEMOUND RD. P.O. BOX 13819 MILWAUKEE, WI 53213

Visit Hal Leonard online at www.halleonard.com

Prices, contents, and availability subject to change without notice.

EASY GUITAR
WITH NOTES & TAB

This series features simplified arrangements with notes, tab, chord charts, and strum and pick patterns.

MIXED FOLIOS

00702002	Acoustic Rock Hits for Easy Guitar	$12.95
00702166	All-Time Best Guitar Collection	$19.99
00699665	Beatles Best	$12.95
00702232	Best Acoustic Songs for Easy Guitar	$12.99
00702233	Best Hard Rock Songs	$14.99
00698978	Big Christmas Collection	$16.95
00702115	Blues Classics	$10.95
00385020	Broadway Songs for Kids	$9.95
00702237	Christian Acoustic Favorites	$12.95
00702149	Children's Christian Songbook	$7.95
00702028	Christmas Classics	$7.95
00702185	Christmas Hits	$9.95
00702016	Classic Blues for Easy Guitar	$12.95
00702141	Classic Rock	$8.95
00702203	CMT's 100 Greatest Country Songs	$27.95
00702170	Contemporary Christian Christmas	$9.95
00702006	Contemporary Christian Favorites	$9.95
00702065	Contemporary Women of Country	$9.95
00702121	Country from the Heart	$9.95
00702240	Country Hits of 2007-2008	$12.95
00702225	Country Hits of '06-'07	$12.95
00702085	Disney Movie Hits	$12.95
00702257	Easy Acoustic Guitar Songs	$14.99
00702212	Essential Christmas	$9.95
00702041	Favorite Hymns for Easy Guitar	$9.95
00702174	God Bless America® & Other Songs for a Better Nation	$8.95
00699374	Gospel Favorites	$14.95
00702160	The Great American Country Songbook	$14.95
00702050	Great Classical Themes for Easy Guitar	$6.95
00702131	Great Country Hits of the '90s	$8.95
00702116	Greatest Hymns for Guitar	$8.95
00702130	The Groovy Years	$9.95
00702184	Guitar Instrumentals	$9.95
00702231	High School Musical for Easy Guitar	$12.95
00702241	High School Musical 2	$12.95
00702249	High School Musical 3	$12.99
00702037	Hits of the '50s for Easy Guitar	$10.95
00702046	Hits of the '70s for Easy Guitar	$8.95
00702032	International Songs for Easy Guitar	$12.95
00702051	Jock Rock for Easy Guitar	$9.95
00702162	Jumbo Easy Guitar Songbook	$19.95
00702112	Latin Favorites	$9.95
00702258	Legends of Rock	$14.99
00702138	Mellow Rock Hits	$10.95
00702147	Motown's Greatest Hits	$9.95
00702039	Movie Themes	$10.95
00702210	Best of MTV Unplugged	$12.95
00702189	MTV's 100 Greatest Pop Songs	$24.95
00702272	1950s Rock	$14.99
00702271	1960s Rock	$14.99
00702270	1970s Rock	$14.99
00702269	1980s Rock	$14.99
00702268	1990s Rock	$14.99
00702187	Selections from O Brother Where Art Thou?	$12.95
00702178	100 Songs for Kids	$12.95
00702158	Songs from Passion	$9.95
00702125	Praise and Worship for Guitar	$9.95
00702155	Rock Hits for Guitar	$9.95
00702242	Rock Band	$19.95
00702256	Rock Band 2	$19.99
00702128	Rockin' Down the Highway	$9.95
00702207	Smash Hits for Guitar	$9.95
00702110	The Sound of Music	$9.99
00702124	Today's Christian Rock – 2nd Edition	$9.95
00702220	Today's Country Hits	$9.95
00702198	Today's Hits for Guitar	$9.95
00702217	Top Christian Hits	$12.95
00702235	Top Christian Hits of '07-'08	$14.95
00702246	Top Hits of 2008	$12.95
00702206	Very Best of Rock	$9.95
00702175	VH1's 100 Greatest Songs of Rock and Roll	$24.95
00702253	Wicked	$12.99
00702192	Worship Favorites	$9.95

ARTIST COLLECTIONS

00702267	AC/DC for Easy Guitar	$14.99
00702001	Best of Aerosmith	$16.95
00702040	Best of the Allman Brothers	$12.95
00702169	Best of The Beach Boys	$10.95
00702201	The Essential Black Sabbath	$12.95
00702140	Best of Brooks & Dunn	$10.95
00702095	Best of Mariah Carey	$12.95
00702043	Best of Johnny Cash	$12.95
00702033	Best of Steven Curtis Chapman	$14.95
00702263	Best of Casting Crowns	$12.99
00702090	Eric Clapton's Best	$10.95
00702086	Eric Clapton – from the Album Unplugged	$10.95
00702202	The Essential Eric Clapton	$12.95
00702250	blink-182 – Greatest Hits	$12.99
00702053	Best of Patsy Cline	$10.95
00702229	The Very Best of Creedence Clearwater Revival	$12.95
00702145	Best of Jim Croce	$10.95
00702219	David Crowder*Band Collection	$12.95
00702122	The Doors for Easy Guitar	$12.99
00702099	Best of Amy Grant	$9.95
00702190	Best of Pat Green	$19.95
00702136	Best of Merle Haggard	$10.95
00702243	Hannah Montana	$14.95
00702244	Hannah Montana 2/Meet Miley Cyrus	$16.95
00702227	Jimi Hendrix – Smash Hits	$14.99
00702236	Best of Antonio Carlos Jobim	$12.95
00702087	Best of Billy Joel	$10.95
00702245	Elton John – Greatest Hits 1970-2002	$14.99
00702204	Robert Johnson	$9.95
00702199	Norah Jones – Come Away with Me	$10.95
00702234	Selections from Toby Keith – 35 Biggest Hits	$12.95
00702003	Kiss	$9.95
00702193	Best of Jennifer Knapp	$12.95
00702097	John Lennon – Imagine	$9.95
00702216	Lynyrd Skynyrd	$14.95
00702182	The Essential Bob Marley	$12.95
00702248	Paul McCartney – All the Best	$14.99
00702129	Songs of Sarah McLachlan	$12.95
02501316	Metallica – Death Magnetic	$15.95
00702209	Steve Miller Band – Young Hearts (Greatest Hits)	$12.95
00702096	Best of Nirvana	$14.95
00702211	The Offspring – Greatest Hits	$12.95
00702030	Best of Roy Orbison	$12.95
00702144	Best of Ozzy Osbourne	$12.95
00702139	Elvis Country Favorites	$9.95
00699415	Best of Queen for Guitar	$14.99
00702208	Red Hot Chili Peppers – Greatest Hits	$12.95
00702093	Rolling Stones Collection	$17.95
00702092	Best of the Rolling Stones	$14.99
00702196	Best of Bob Seger	$12.95
00702252	Frank Sinatra – Nothing But the Best	$12.99
00702010	Best of Rod Stewart	$14.95
00702150	Best of Sting	$12.95
00702049	Best of George Strait	$12.95
00702259	Taylor Swift for Easy Guitar	$12.99
00702223	Chris Tomlin – Arriving	$12.95
00702262	Chris Tomlin Collection	$14.99
00702226	Chris Tomlin – See the Morning	$12.95
00702132	Shania Twain – Greatest Hits	$10.95
00702108	Best of Stevie Ray Vaughan	$10.95
00702123	Best of Hank Williams	$9.95
00702111	Stevie Wonder – Guitar Collection	$9.95
00702228	Neil Young – Greatest Hits	$12.99
00702188	Essential ZZ Top	$10.95

Prices, contents and availability subject to change without notice.

FOR MORE INFORMATION, SEE YOUR LOCAL MUSIC DEALER,
OR WRITE TO:

HAL•LEONARD®
CORPORATION
7777 W. BLUEMOUND RD. P.O. BOX 13819 MILWAUKEE, WI 53213
Visit Hal Leonard online at **www.halleonard.com**

0610

Must-Have Collections
for Every Guitarist!

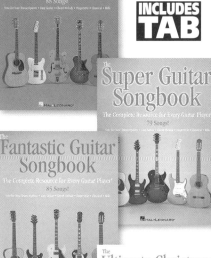

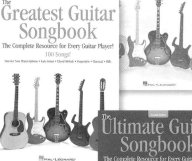

INCLUDES TAB

The Definitive Guitar Songbook

There's something for every guitarist in this amazing collection! It features 88 songs in all styles of music and all forms of notation, including: Guitar Recorded Versions (Birthday • Ramblin' Man); Easy Guitar with Notes & Tab (Blackbird • Don't Be Cruel); Easy Guitar (Baby Love • Cheek to Cheek • Young Americans); Chord Melody Guitar (I Could Write a Book • When I Fall in Love); Classical Guitar (Gavotte • Prelude); Fingerstyle Guitar (Imagine • My One and Only Love); and Guitar Riffs (Fire and Rain • Maggie May • Twist and Shout).

00699267 Guitar Collection $19.95

The Fantastic Guitar Songbook

85 tunes in a wide variety of notation formats (easy guitar with and without tablature, chord melody guitar, classical, fingerstyle, riffs and note-for-note tab transcriptions), and in a range of musical styles – from pop/rock hits to jazz standards, movie songs to Motown, country, classical and everything in between. Includes: ABC • Canon in D • Drops of Jupiter • Hey Jude • I Am a Man of Constant Sorrow • Jack and Diane • Leader of the Band • Mama, I'm Coming Home • Summer of '69 • So Nice (Summer Samba) • Tush • We've Only Just Begun • Yellow Submarine • and more.

00699561 Guitar Collection $19.95

The Greatest Guitar Songbook

This comprehensive collection for all guitarists includes 100 songs in genres from jazz standards, to pop/rock favorites, Motown masterpieces and movie music, to traditional tunes, country numbers and classical pieces. Notation styles include: note-for-note transcriptions (Sweet Child O' Mine • Wild Thing); Easy Guitar with Notes & Tab (Day Tripper • Für Elise • Misty); Easy Guitar (Boot Scootin' Boogie • Unchained Melody); Fingerstyle Guitar (Amazing Grace • Greensleeves); and Guitar Riffs (Angie • Layla • My Girl); and more!

00699142 Guitar Collection $20.95

The Incredible Guitar Songbook

Features a whopping 111 songs in genres from blues to jazz to pop and rock to classical and country, and a variety of notation styles, including: Note-for-note transcriptions in notes and tab (Tears in Heaven • Wonderwall); Easy Guitar with Notes and Tab (All Shook Up • Bésame Mucho • Pride and Joy); Easy Guitar, No Tab (Michelle • Route 66); Chord Melody Guitar (Satin Doll); Classical Guitar (Bourée • Pavane); Fingerstyle Guitar (Something); and Guitar Riffs (Beast of Burden • Gloria).

00699245 Guitar Collection $19.95

The Phenomenal Guitar Songbook

This remarkable book features 85 songs from all styles of music. It includes a variety of note-for-note transcriptions, riffs, and arrangements for easy guitar, chord melody, fingerstyle, and classical guitar. Songs include: Ain't Too Proud to Beg • Blue Skies • California Dreamin' • Fly like an Eagle • Fur Elise • Giant Steps • God Bless the U.S.A. • Good Vibrations • Green Onions • In My Life • Moon River • My Way • Proud Mary • Redneck Woman • Under the Bridge • What's Going On • You Are My Sunshine • and more!

00699759 Guitar Collection $19.99

The Super Guitar Songbook

The latest songbook in our wildly popular series of mixed collections of guitar arrangements and transcriptions. This book features 79 songs in a wide variety of music styles and notation formats: Guitar Recorded Versions, fingerstyle, easy guitar with notes and tab, classical, chord melody, and riffs! These books truly grow with the player! Songs include: Bewitched • California Girls • Come to My Window • (Everything I Do) I Do It for You • In a Sentimental Mood • Lucy in the Sky with Diamonds • Oye Como Va • Rocky Top • Scuttle Buttin' • Sharp Dressed Man • Soul Man • You'll Be in My Heart • and more!

00699618 Guitar Collection $19.99

The Ultimate Christmas Guitar Songbook

100 songs in a variety of notation styles, from easy guitar and classical guitar arrangements to note-for-note guitar tab transcriptions. Includes: All Through the Night • Auld Lang Syne • Blue Christmas • The Chipmunk Song • The Gift • (There's No Place Like) Home for the Holidays • I've Got My Love to Keep Me Warm • Jingle Bells • My Favorite Things • One Bright Star • Rockin' Around the Christmas Tree • Santa Baby • Silver Bells • Wonderful Christmastime • and more.

00700185 Guitar Collection $19.95

The Ultimate Guitar Songbook – Second Edition

110 songs in all genres and guitar styles: everything from pop/rock hits to jazz standards, Motown masterpieces to movie classics, traditional tunes, country favorites, Broadway blockbusters and beyond! Features note-for-note transcriptions, riffs, and arrangements for easy guitar, chord melody, fingerstyle, classical & more!

00699909 Guitar Collection $19.99

The Ultra Guitar Songbook

The latest edition in our popular series featuring multiple notation styles, perfect for players looking for a little variety in their playing! This collection features 87 songs in Guitar Recorded Versions notation (Bad Moon Rising • Hot for Teacher); Easy Guitar (Bennie and the Jets • Free Fallin' • Ring of Fire • Tainted Love); Chord Melody Guitar (Come Fly with Me • Witchcraft); Classical Guitar (Capricho Arabe • Minuet in G); Fingerstyle Guitar (Every Rose Has Its Thorn • Fields of Gold); Guitar Riffs (Beautiful Girls • Dancing with Myself); and many more!

00700130 Guitar Collection $19.95

Prices, contents, and availability
subject to change without notice.

FOR MORE INFORMATION, SEE YOUR LOCAL MUSIC DEALER,
OR WRITE TO:

HAL•LEONARD®
CORPORATION
7777 W. BLUEMOUND RD. P.O. BOX 13819 MILWAUKEE, WI 53213

www.halleonard.com

0210